MONOGRAPHS ON GREENLAND
MEDDELELSER OM GRØNLAND
Vol. 53, no. 4

FACSIMILE
EDITION

Thomas Thomsen

The Angmagsalik Eskimo

Notes and Corrections to Vol. 39 of Monographs on Greenland

MUSEUM TUSCULANUM PRESS
UNIVERSITY OF COPENHAGEN
2010

Thomas Thomsen
The Angmagsalik Eskimo
Notes and Corrections to Vol. 39 of Monographs on Greenland

Facsimile Edition © Museum Tusculanum Press, 2010
Cover design: Erling Lynder
ISBN 978 87 635 2269 4
eISBN 978 87 635 3458 1

Original print edition, Copenhagen, 1917

Monographs on Greenland | Meddelelser om Grønland
Vol. 53, no. 4
ISSN 0025 6676

www.mtp.dk/MoG

Published with financial support from
The Commission for Scientific Research in Greenland.

Museum Tusculanum Press
University of Copenhagen
126 Njalsgade, DK-2300 Copenhagen S
DENMARK
www.mtp.dk

MONOGRAPHS ON GREENLAND | MEDDELELSER OM GRØNLAND

ABOUT THE SERIES

Monographs on Greenland | Meddelelser om Grønland (ISSN 0025 6676) has published scientific results from all fields of research on Greenland since 1878. The series numbers more than 345 volumes comprising more than 1250 titles.

In 1979 Monographs on Greenland | Meddelelser om Grønland was developed into a tripartite series consisting of Bioscience (ISSN 0106-1054), Man & Society (ISSN 0106-1062), and Geoscience (ISSN 0106-1046).

Monographs on Greenland | Meddelelser om Grønland was renumbered in 1979 ending with volume no. 206 and continued with volume no. 1 for each subseries. As of 2008 the original Monographs on Greenland | Meddelelser om Grønland numbering is continued in addition to the subseries numbering.

Further information about the series, including addresses of the scientific editors of the subseries, can be found at www.mtp.dk/MoG.

MANUSCRIPTS SHOULD BE SENT TO

Museum Tusculanum Press
University of Copenhagen
126 Njalsgade, DK-2300 Copenhagen S
DENMARK
info@mtp.dk | www.mtp.dk
Tel. +45 353 29109 | Fax +45 353 29113
VAT no.: 8876 8418

ORDERS

Books can be purchased online at www.mtp.dk, via order@mtp.dk, through any of our distributors in the US, UK, and France or via online retailers and major booksellers. Museum Tusculanum Press bank details: Amagerbanken, DK-2300 Copenhagen S, BIC: AM BK DK KK, IBAN: DK10 5202 0001 5151 08.

DISTRIBUTORS

USA & Canada: ISBS International Specialized Book Services, 920 NE 58th Ave. Suite 300 - Portland, OR 97213, Phone: +1 800 944 6190 (toll-free), Fax: +1 503 280 8832, orders@isbs.com

United Kingdom: Gazelle Book Services Ltd., White Cross Mills, High Town, GB-Lancaster LA1 4XS, United Kingdom, Phone: +44 1524 68765, Fax: +44 1524 63232, sales@gazellebooks.co.uk

France: Editions Picard, 82, rue Bonaparte, F-75006 Paris, France, Phone: +33 (0) 1 4326 9778, Fax: +33 1 43 26 42 64, livres@librairie-picard.fr

IV.

THE ANGMAGSALIK ESKIMO

NOTES AND CORRECTIONS TO VOL. XXXIX OF MEDDELELSER OM GRØNLAND

BY

THOMAS THOMSEN

I N the year 1884, GUSTAV HOLM, then First Lieutenant in the Danish
Navy, landed in the Angmagsalik district for the purpose of wintering
among an Eskimo tribe, concerning which nothing was known in Europe
at that time. The event forms something of an epoch in the history
of Danish arctic investigation. The discovery of Angmagsalik opened
up a new and important field for research: the tribe in question, living
untouched by civilisation, had retained much which the Eskimos of
Western Greenland had discarded during the course of close upon 200
years of Danish influence, and had, on the other hand, developed in
their isolation various peculiarities unknown to their kindred on the west.

There was much to do, and much was done, that winter in Angmagsalik: an extensive collection illustrative of native culture was brought
home in the following year, and the results of the winter's work were
set forth in an exhaustive treatise[1], cleverly and brightly written, and
illustrated with numerous plates, the appearance of which deservedly
aroused considerable remark.

Despite the care and acumen exhibited in gathering together the
original collection (now preserved in the National Museum at Copenhagen) the material nevertheless naturally needed to be augmented here
and there. Such supplementary material was also furnished, in considerable quantity, by C. RYDER, who stayed for some time at Angmagsalik
in September 1892, on his return from the expedition to Scoresby Sound[2].

A further unique addition was made to the collection by G. AM-
DRUP's Expedition, 1898—1900. At Nualik, north of Angmagsalik,
Lat. 67°15′5″ N.) the travellers came upon a house with furnishings and
gear intact, while skeletal remains of the inmates scattered about outside seemed to suggest that the entire family had perished simultaneously
by some mischance, in all probability poison. On coming in to Angmagsalik, Capt. AMDRUP showed some of the implements found to natives

---

[1] G. HOLM: Ethnologisk Skizze af Angmagsalikerne. 1887. (Meddelelser om
Grønland vol. 10.)

[2] Cf. Meddelelser om Grønland vol. 17, p. 138 ff.

there, who recognised the things as having belonged to a party which had set out to the northward in 1882, and had never returned[1].

These three collections together serve to illustrate the culture of Angmagsalik at about the time of its discovery.

In 1894, a new stage in the development of the place was reached, a Danish trading station and mission settlement being then established there. Since that time, the trading interest has been superintended by one man, Kolonibestyrer Johan Petersen, who had himself been one of the members of the Holm expedition. Keenly interested in ethnographical work, Hr. Johan Petersen has repeatedly rendered valuable service to the National Museum, not only by procuring specified objects which it was desirable to acquire, but also by personally tendering independent contributions. The Mission authorities also took an interest in the work, and both Pastor C. Rüttel and his successor, Kr. Rosing, have furnished material of great value, and hardly obtainable from other quarters, such as for instance the collection of amulets given up by newly baptised Eskimos; Pastor Rosing's collection of these is particularly valuable, on account of the detailed information with which it is supplemented.

Finally, a small collection, the result of a winter's stay in 1905—06, was furnished by Cand. W. Thalbitzer.

In this series of collections, together with such minor additions as have been made from time to time, the National Museum possesses a remarkably complete equipment illustrative of the material culture of Angmagsalik from the time of its discovery in 1884 to the present day; the finds relative to older times, however, are very few.

Since the publication of Holm's work, no scientific treatise dealing with this extensive collection has appeared. The task was one of considerable magnitude, and the announcement of a forthcoming volume on the subject, the cost of which was to be defrayed by the Carlsberg Fund, naturally aroused no little interest. The first portion of this work has now appeared, forming Vol. 39 of Meddelelser om Grønland[2], an imposing volume, of no less than 755 pages, with illustrations amounting to 398 separate figures, the number of objects depicted being considerable more.

The work is thus abundantly illustrated; on perusal, however, it is at once evident that both the illustrations and the accompanying text stand strongly in need of some explanatory supplement or guide. The task of furnishing this last devolves, naturally enough, upon the National Museum, being a matter of plain duty towards the gentlemen

---

[1] Meddelelser om Grønland vol. 28, p. 310.

[2] The Ammassalik Eskimo. Contributions to the Ethnology of the East Greenland. Edited by William Thalbitzer. First Part. (This work is quoted in the following pages as Thalb. II.)

who have entrusted their collections to its care, as well as towards the science of which such collections form the principal foundation. It will be necessary, moreover, in the course of the work, to make various additions concerning different portions of the subject-matter.

PLAN AND CONTENTS OF THE WORK.

At a cursory glance, it appears somewhat difficult to obtain a clear idea as to the contents of the work. According to the Title Page, the work should contain "the ethnological and anthropological results of G. HOLM's expedition in 1883—85 and G. AMDRUP's expedition in 1898—1900". The Preface states that the volume combines "the ethnographic results of three Danish expeditions to East Greenland", namely, in addition to the two already mentioned, "W. THALBITZER's voyage and wintering at Ammassalik in 1905—06". On examination of the actual Contents we find, that the six first chapters (317 pages) consist of an English translation of G. HOLM's work already mentioned, and the papers published in connection therewith in Vol. 10 of Medd. om Grønland. The work has been partially revised, and augmented with some new matter: to HOLM's work, for instance, a description of the journey has here been added, together with some new reproductions, while on the other hand, most of the illustrations pertaining to the HOLM collection have been removed from their place, and new reproductions of the same objects included in Chapter VII.

The six first chapters are thus, in all essentials, a translation of previously printed work of acknowledged value. The seventh and last, which comprises the greater part of the book, is composed of entirely new matter. The first chapters having dealt with HOLM's expedition, one might naturally expect the last to give the promised ethnological and anthropological results of the AMDRUP expedition, or, trusting to the words of the Preface, one might even hope to find those of THALBITZER's as well; the title of Part VII, however, mentions only the ethnographical collections made by G. HOLM, G. AMDRUP and J. PETERSEN. The anthropologist who had hoped to find there G. AMDRUP's anthropological results will thus be disappointed, while the ethnographer, on the other hand, will be pleasantly surprised to find that the promised number of collections has been increased by one, viz; JOHAN PETERSEN's; he will also, on perusing the part in question, find both the "Grønlandske Administration's" and W. THALBITZER's collections represented.

The confusion which is thus apparent in the plan of the work as a whole is, however, by no means inherent in the task entrusted to the Editor, which was briefly and plainly this: to describe the AMDRUP ethnographical collection. The first part of this work was already done[1]; all that remained was, practically speaking, to describe the find made at Nualik already referred to. The unique quantity of material thus obtained from a single house furnished an excellent basis for a valuable piece of work on the culture of the Angmagsalik Eskimo at the time immediately previous to the Danish occupation. This task, however, interesting though it might seem in itself, failed to satisfy our Editor, who "laid before the Commission .... a plan of wider scope, in accordance with which the description of Amdrup's collection was to be published jointly with an English edition of Holm's Ethnological Sketch of the Angmagsalik Eskimo, along with the anthropological papers which had appeared in ‚Meddelelser om Grønland' as the results of his famous expedition, and with new illustrations of his collection"[2]. And it is beyond question that Holm's work, which was out of print, well deserved to be issued in a new edition, calculated to reach a wider circle of readers, and illustrated with modern reproductions on a larger scale, and more generally representative of the collection, in place of the crude lithographs which had served the purpose of the original work. With these two widely different tasks before him, then: to describe a collection, and to compile a new edition of a series of previously published papers, the Editor set to work.

Still insatiate, however, as it would seem, he continued to drag in new matter, which, gradually mounting up, threatened to submerge the original plan altogether: Amdrup's interesting find, the principal value of which lay in the fact of its forming a single whole, is cut up into scattered illustrations, with no attempt at special and collective treatment, while the new illustrations prepared for Holm's work are removed from their place in the same and strewn, together with those of Amdrup's and many other collections, throughout the mentioned Part VII.

The inadvisability of such a method of treatment will easily be realised. Holm's treatise appears no longer as an independent work, but as an appendix to that which forms the subject of the present observations. Its unity even is destroyed, while the illustrations with which it now appears have been drawn from different collections varying considerably in point of time and place. And finally, the Editor has not succeeded in dissociating the English translation from the original Danish edition, to which, albeit the work is no longer ordinarily procurable, reference is not infrequently made for illustrations.

---

[1] Ethnological description of the Amdrup Collection from East Greenland. Cop. 1909 (Medd. om Grønland vol. 28). This part of the work will be dealt with later on. It is referred to in the following pages as Thalb. I.

[2] Cf. Thalb. II, p. I—II.

TREATMENT OF THE MUSEUM MATERIAL.

Prior to the commencement of his task, the Author was acquainted with the Museum "only as a general visitor" and found it "almost impossible .... to see what is placed at the back" of the cases[1]. Later on, however, his interest in Museums increased: "I began to take more pleasure in the collections of Museums than before; the dead objects assumed life and personality. From the silent cases I began to hear the language and thoughts of the people"[2]. Nevertheless, after having photographed here as much as he pleased ("the work .... extended over 16 days") he felt "no inducement to continue" his studies of the objects removed from their cases for his examination. The reader will doubtless be disposed to acquiesce in Mr. THALBITZER's statement as to the "strength" of the work having been "reduced" thereby[3].

So completely, indeed, did the Author relinquish his studies at the Museum, that he did not even make any enquiry as to the origin of the objects which he had selected and photographed; had he but handed in a list of the numbers, with a request for particulars of each, the result would, as will subsequently be seen, have increased the value of the work to no slight degree.

Mr. THALBITZER has himself, albeit somewhat tardily, realised to a certain extent the disability thus involved. On the last page of the work, under the heading of "Corrigenda", he mentions that "in several of the objects ... designated ... as belonging to the HOLM collection doubts may be raised whether they really belong to this collection, or originate from GRAAH's journey, or have been added on later occasions, e. g. sent by J. PETERSEN from Ammassalik". The Author feels some uncertainty in this respect regarding ten illustrations in the text. "On the other hand", we read, "the nondescript objects shown in fig. 241 (p. 517) surely belong to the HOLM collection"[4].

Such an observation can scarcely fail to produce a discouraging effect upon the reader, who is thus suddenly confronted with the possibility that certain objects are not from Angmagsalik at all, while others may be of far later date than HOLM's collection. To anyone in doubt on such a matter, the self-evident course would surely be: to ask. And the fact that the Author has not seen fit to adopt this obvious expedient is hardly calculated to inspire confidence. As it is, the Museum must now take upon itself the task of correctly stating the origin of the objects in question.

---

[1] THALB. II, pp. 328 and 325—26.
[2] l. c., p. 327.
[3] THALB. II, p. 329. The fact that the Editor seeks to lay this lack of interest on his part to the charge of the Museum should not be regarded as of any great importance. As will be seen in the following, his work elsewhere is subject to the same inconstancy.
[4] l. c., p. 755.

That Mr. THALBITZER regards the objects shown in Fig. 241 as "surely" belonging to the HOLM collection is hardly to be wondered at, since the implements in question are drawn in Plate XIX of HOLM's "Ethnologisk Skizze". On the other hand, his doubt as regards Fig. 190 is unfounded, which is just as well, in view of the fact that HOLM's name appears here, not only beneath the illustration, but also in the text.

Of the remainder, the greater part, viz; Figs. 172b, 314c, 314d, 315b, 315c, and 327b, belong to C. RYDER's collection, Fig. 334 is from that of JOHAN PETERSEN, while Nos. 273 and 309 represent objects brought in during the years 1849—54.

Doubts having thus arisen as to the correctness of the descriptions given, the Museum authorities found it advisable to go through the whole list of the objects stated as belonging to the HOLM collection[1], which piece of work was amply justified by the results. It was found that the Author ought, as a matter of fact, to have included in his "doubtful" category a great deal more than the ten items to which he refers. True, this would have involved the necessity of expanding the note in question to an inconvenient length, since the items attributed to HOLM include, in actual fact:

79 objects brought home by C. RYDER in 1892. This considerable collection, numerically superior to HOLM's, can hardly have been unknown to Mr. THALBITZER — RYDER's name is mentioned on p. 325 — he appears, however, to have disregarded it altogether save when borrowing therefrom large quantities of material which he ascribes to the HOLM collection.

44 objects collected at different times by JOHAN PETERSEN.

13 belonging to the proceeds of W. THALBITZER's voyage in 1905—06, making about one-eighth of that collection. And this moreover, despite the fact that the Editor must be supposed to have had a certain acquaintance with the objects in question, since he gives a list of them on p. 752.

2 brought home by Pastor C. RÜTTEL, 1 anonymously contributed in 1894; 10 dating from the years 1838—65 and 2 from 1881.

We thus find that no less than 151, or two-fifths of the total number of objects attributed to HOLM, are in reality derived from other collections.

Here and there, it is true, the Author is at some pains to be more exact, in the figures marked "HOLM and later collections".

This designation, however, certainly appears somewhat remarkable when, as in Fig. 352, it applies to but a single object, this being, moreover, from C. RYDER's collection. It is equally misleading in the case

---

[1] In a few instances it has proved impossible to identify the objects as shown in the illustrations; possibly some of them may not be from the National Museum at all.

of Fig. 351, the three amulets there shown being all — as any ordinary visitor to the Museum might see from the labels attached — brought home by Pastor C. Rüttel, together with those marked c, d, e and f in Fig. 350.

Two pieces in the last-named figure, however, viz. a. and b. are from Holm's collection. As regards a, we are informed in a note[1]: "The same object is seen in the illustration on p. 45". There is no illustration of this — or of anything else — on p. 45; we do find, however, in Fig. 45 on p. 117, a far better reproduction than the second edition on p. 632. Fig. 350b was found by Holm in a grave at Ungudlik in the Julianehaab district, and is thus outside the sphere of the work in question.

This action of the Author in calmly attributing to the Holm collection some hundred and fifty objects cannot be passed over by the Museum without comment, more particularly since the objects in question are taken from the collections of others. The men who have entrusted the results of their work to the care of the Museum would have good grounds for complaint on seeing their best items reproduced in a publication as belonging to another[2]. The Museum authorities, it need hardly be said, regard it as their duty towards research to afford anyone seeking material for scientific work the fullest liberty to make requisite search and selection of material; it is nevertheless an equally obvious duty to watch over the interests of the collectors in such cases as the present.

Apart from this, however, energetic protest must also be made on behalf of the science of ethnography itself, which forms part of the Museum's sphere of work.

The name of G. Holm is permanently connected with the discovery of Angmagsalik, and future research will very justifiably take the reproductions of his collection as representative of the culture of Angmagsalik in 1884, when the natives were first brought into direct contact with

---

[1] Thalb. II, p. 633.

[2] It is unfortunately hardly probable that even this correction will entirely suffice to obviate the consequence of the inaccuracy. A characteristic instance for the difficulty experienced in repairing an error once published is furnished by the case of E. W. Nelson's "The Eskimo about Bering Strait". In the course of printing, the texts beneath two of the plates were unfortunately transposed. The author did what he could to prevent the threatened confusion by inserting a slip in the work, with the necessary correction, to be pasted under the figures in question. Nevertheless we find that W. Thalbitzer, in a work of popular character published in Sweden, entitled "Grønlandske Sagn om Eskimoernes Fortid" (p. 56) reproduces one of these plates with the erroneous text: "Eskimo from Alaska throwing a bird dart" the man in the picture having a seal spear in his hand. Such an error is naturally not likely to be further propagated by writers having any knowledge of the difference between these two common weapons; works are, however, frequently published by men having no very intimate acquaintance with the subjects of which they treat, whereby mistakes are circulated abroad.

the Danes. It is thus not a matter of slight moment that 60 of the objects thus described were brought home subsequently to the foundation of the Danish trading station there, not a few changes having taken place since HOLM's day[1]. A still graver fault, however, is the inclusion of half a score of objects which do not originate from Angmagsalik at all, but from the west coast, brought thither by natives from the east (all with one exception being from the south-east coast) before the discovery of Angmagsalik, for the most part as far back as 1839—65.

By way of example we may take Fig. 293 (p. 567) "Women's inner breeches". None of these are from HOLM's time; a. was received from JOHAN PETERSEN in 1908, b. from RYDER in 1892; both are, however, characteristic pieces of Angmagsalik work, whereas c. and d. were brought over by way of the West Coast in 1865 and 1846 respectively, and may easily be distinguished from the first two; d. especially is ornamented with a pattern entirely foreign to the style of dress in Angmagsalik.

We need not, however, peer into the future for possible harmful effects of our Author's carelessness; the work itself already exhibits instances of error arising from the incorrect designation of the objects shown in the illustrations.

Thus in Fig. 392, (p. 667) the subjoined text ascribes to the HOLM collection a kind of wooden calendar, brought home in 1848 and then described as originating from Eastern Greenland, not from Angmagsalik, the very name of which was then unknown.

In the Danish edition of HOLM's work[2] we find the following passage with regard to the reckoning of time then current in Angmagsalik: "Division by weeks is of course unknown. HANSERAK made an almanach of the kind used on the West coast, i. e. made of wood and having seven holes, in which a peg is placed for every day in the week. We gave this almanach to Ilinguaki, in order that during the winter, when he lived far from us, he might be able to know when it was our Sunday. When we came to Ilinguaki next year, we found that he had been using it constantly".

The note in question is translated in W. THALBITZER's English edition, reference being made to Fig. 392[3]. Cand. THALBITZER must therefore have regarded the almanack shown in fig. 392 as the one made by HANSERAK for a special purpose.

Our examination of the material has been restricted to the objects photographed in the Museum, and therefore does not include the illustrations from AMDRUP's and JOHAN PETERSEN's collections, which were not deposited in the Museum until a later date. The examination revealed a number of other faults and omissions, such as incorrect indication of the scale of reproduction, query mark after the scale as given, inclusion

---

[1] cf. the Editor's own words l. c. p. 387 and p. 579.
[2] Medd. om Grønland, vol. 10, p. 141 footnote.
[3] THALB. II, p. 105.

of models and toy weapons among real implements intended for use, without any statement as to this being the case, and erroneous statements as to the material of which the objects were made. To avoid wearying the reader with unnecessary quotations, we may here once and for all refer to the list given in the following (p. 426 ff.) of such mistakes as have been discovered. Only such errors as demand more detailed treatment will be specially dealt with here.

TREATMENT OF THE AUTHORITIES QUOTED.

If the extent to which the Author has had recourse to the Museum is but slight, it must be admitted that the number of previously published works called into requisition for the compilation of the volume in question is by no means inconsiderable. The Author even devotes a separate chapter to consideration of the older literature concerning the Eskimo of Davis Straits[1]. This is perhaps somewhat of a digression from the actual object of the work, but will doubtless be welcomed by foreign readers, to whom the unpublished part at least of such documents would hardly be known. And for this very reason it is extremely likely that the chapter in question will be frequently quoted. It may therefore not be out of place to offer some remarks as to the four least known works there referred to.

With regard to OLEARIUS, Mr. THALBITZER states[2] that "the three Greenlanders brought to Copenhagen .. were sent to the king .... at Gottorp". In Note 2 on the same page, we read that "a contemporary painting of the four Greenlanders going from Greenland via Throndhjem, where the picture was painted, to Copenhagen, is found in the National Museum of Copenhagen".

This discrepancy in the figures, at which the reader naturally wonders, is due to the fact that one of the Greenlanders in question, the only male of the party, died on the way from Norway, and thus never reached Copenhagen at all. With regard to this note, it only remains to add that the king was not at Gottorp, but at Flensborg, whence he gave orders for the three Greenlanders to be sent to the Duke of Gottorp, "weil selbige auch sonderlich belieben tragen zu sehen, was Gott und die Natur an so fern abgelegenen Orten gibt und zeuget". The party had, moreover, travelled, not by way of Throndhjem, but via Bergen, where the picture was painted — which fact, by the way, the Author has himself referred to in an earlier part of the work[3].

The next work quoted is DE POINCY's report of NICOLAS TUNES'

---

[1] THALB. II, p. 682—85.
[2] l. c. p. 682.
[3] l. c. p. 436.

voyage to Davis Straits in 1656[1]. We are informed by Mr. Thalbitzer that he "landed at 64°10′ N. lat., whether on Baffin Land or Green-land is not clear"[2]. On consulting the original, however, we find that he entered a fjord (rivière) at this latitude, and sailed thence north-ward as far as the 72nd degree, "where lies that land now to be described".

With regard to De Poincy's description of the native dress, Cand. Thalbitzer regards his statement to the effect that the women do not wear ear drops as "possibly .... due to lack of observation, for he says, namely, that they wear neither bracelets nor necklaces nor ear-drops but are decorated by tattoo-markings on the cheeks". The suggestion as to "lack of observation" appears somewhat peculiar, in view of the fact that the passage quoted contains a distinct negation, together with a number of positive observations[3]. And when Mr. Thalbitzer opines that it is "hardly possible that the use of bracelets should be unknown among them at the place and during the time of De Poincy's obser-vations" it should be remembered, that he has in the first place located the "place" in question under a wrong latitude, nearly 8° too far south, and further, that he does not even know on which side of Davis Straits it lies. De Poincy expressly states that the Dutch mariner set out in search of new trading grounds[4] in the northern lands, so that he is hardly likely to have followed the usual route. The word "Observa-tion" by the way, should naturally not be taken literally here: De Poincy, as we know, did not see these things with his own eyes at all, but received his information from the Dutch Captain[5].

The next source drawn upon by Cand. Thalbitzer is the Manu-script of Matthias Schacht, referred to in the "List of works consulted" as N. Kgl. S. 4° 1965 (and A. M. 364 Fol. and A. M. 775, 4°) Kbhvn. 1789. He quotes from this work on p. 635, where we find, in Note 2: "Schacht, (1789, but his MS written before 1700, when he died), p. 263".

In order to remove something of the difficulty which the reader would otherwise encounter in seeking out the source in question, we may at once observe that the information referred to will not be found in the MS. N. Kgl. Saml. 4to 1965, this being a copy made at the close of the 18th century, which breaks off abruptly in the middle of Chap. 22. Equally fruitless would it be to consult the alternative MS, A. M. 775 4to, this copy likewise terminating in the same chapter.

---

[1] In the list of works consulted, this is stated as in "chapter the 8th on Davis Straits". As a matter of fact, the chapter in question is the 18th.

[2] Thalb. II, p. 683.

[3] De Poincy even adds: "Mais pour tout ornement elles se font une taillade en chaque joue".

[4] "Decouvrir quelque nouveau commerce".

[5] The chapter in question has been previously translated into English; vide David Mac Ritchie: The Eskimos of Davis Strait in 1656 (Scottish Geo-graphical Magazine for June 1912).

There remains then no other source but the principal MS, A. M. 364 Fol.[1] True, the entire text of the work in question consists of but 192 written pages, of which, again, only 169 are numbered, so that p. 263 does not exist; the quotation in question will, however, be found on p. 166. It is unnecessary, by the way, to guess at the age of this MS, as it is fully dated[2]. We may, on the other hand, hazard a guess that it is the date of compilation of the MS. 1689 which has betrayed Mr. THALBITZER into quoting the year 1789. MATTHIAS SCHACHT, by the way, gives, at the commencement of his work, a long list of writers, which Mr. THALBITZER would have done well to make use of, when attempting to give a synopsis of early works on the subject of Greenland.

On pp. 635—36, the Editor quotes OLEARIUS and SCHACHT in evidence of the use of wooden dolls as idols in western Greenland in the 17th century. Mr. THALBITZER here states as follows: "Some idols of this kind were brought to Copenhagen probably by the Dannell expedition in 1654".

The passage in OLEARIUS from which this is taken runs as follows:

"Was der Grünländer Religion anlanget, hat man nicht erfahren können, wie es darumb beschaffen. Sie seynd ausser Zweyfel Heyden, und Götzendiener, wie dann einen solchen Götzen, welcher in der Strasse Davis vom Lande genommen, wir aus Paludanus Kunst Cammer bekommen. Ist aus Holtz grob geschnitzet, einer halben Ellen lang, mit Federn- und Haarfell bekleidet und mit kleinen lenglichten Thier Zahnen behenget" etc.[3].

This statement has been entirely misunderstood by Cand. THALBITZER and needs explanation. OLEARIUS' "wir" refers to the "Kunstkammer" at Gottorp, where he filled the office of librarian and antiquary. PALUDANUS is the Dutch physician BERNHARDUS PALUDANUS, whose "Kunstkammer" at Enckhuisen was celebrated in its time[4]. He died in 1633, aged 83, and the collection was subsequently sold by this heirs to Duke Frederik III of Gottorp, forming the nucleus of the ducal Kunstkammer. It was fetched by OLEARIUS in person in 1651[5].

OLEARIUS, then, speaks not of several objects, but of one. This one was brought to Gottorp, not to Copenhagen, and brought, moreover, not from Western Greenland by DANNELL in 1654, but from some place

---

[1] As AM. 364 Fol. the MS. is cited also in P. LAURIDSEN: Bibliographia Groenlandica (Medd. om Grønl. vol. 13).

[2] Dabam Cartemindæ Septimo Calend. Maji Anni post reparatam salutem MDCLXXXIX.

[3] OLEARIUS p. 176 (cit. THALB. II, p. 683, Note 2).

[4] GEERART BRANDT: Beschriewing en Lof der Stad Enkhuisen. Blad 25—29, and A. I. VAN DER AA: Biographisch Wordenbook der Nederlanden.

[5] OLEARIUS: Gottorfische Kunstkammer, introduction.

near Davis Straits to Holland, at any rate before 1633, and probably considerably earlier.

Failing, then, to find Cand. Thalbitzer's Copenhagen idols in Olearius' work, we may proceed to seek for them in that of Schacht. He however, evidently has his information from Olearius and no other; he gives a reproduction of the wooden figure from the Gottorp Museum, and quotes the substance of Olearius' report, not, it is true, the place quoted by Mr. Thalbitzer, from the Persian journey, but that mentioned by Schacht himself; viz: Gottorfische Kunstkammer Tab. IV, No. 5. The text here is as follows: "Num. 5. Ist ein Abgott der Nordländer bey der Straat Davis, umb welchen sie, wie die Grünländer, denen ich es gezeigt, berichteten, herumb tantzen. Ist bekleidet mit rauchem Schaaffell, Vogelfedern, und mit kleinen Zähnen von Fischen behangen. Denn sie meynen, weil sie von den drey Elementen ihre Nahrung haben, mussen selbige auch als Götter geehret werden; wie noch jetzo die Heyden im Königreich Siam in Ostindien thun" etc. It will be noticed that Olearius has here improved upon the former simple statement, by adding his theory of the three elements. Schacht follows him faithfully in this, and further declares the figure to be of Greenlandic origin, — which is more than Olearius directly states — and proceeds, on his own account, to draw comparisons with Priapus and other phallic deities. Cand. Thalbitzer again, does not consider the phallic element sufficiently pronounced in the figure in question, which induces him to "draw the conclusion that he" — i. e. Schacht — "speaks of another similar wooden doll in the Gottorp Museum" that is to say, one other than that which he shows in his illustration; a somewhat daring hypothesis.

The next and last source is "The Royal Private-Museum, which was for some time lodged at the Gottorp Castle" and "described by Jacobæus in his Theatrum regium".

It should here be noted that the title of the work in question is "Museum Regium" and that the Royal Museum never was "lodged at Gottorp". The Duke Frederik just referred to had there laid the foundation of his own collection; under his successors, however, relations between the ducal house of Gottorp and the King grew more and more strained, until finally, in 1721, the Gottorp estates in Slesvig were appropriated by the Crown. The Gottorp collection was subsequently, (abt. 1750) removed to Copenhagen and included in the Royal Museum[1].

---

[1] In David Murray's "Museums, their history and their use", Glasgow 1904, Vol. 1, p. 96, we read: "The whole of the Gottorp collection ultimately found its way to St. Petersburg, and was absorbed in the Imperial collection". Upon what grounds this assertion is based I do not know: it is a fact. however, that in 1743, an "Inventarium ueber die Kunst- uud Naturalien Cammer des Schlosses Gottorff", was drawn up at Gottorp Castle, the inventory in question being a catalogue of the collection as transferred to Copenhagen, in the collections of which city many of the original specimens from Gottorp may still be identified.

It is presumably this last fact which Mr. THALBITZER must have had in mind; he has merely, reversed the facts. This erroneous idea is doubtless likewise responsible for his explanation as to the Copenhagen dolls.

These four sources, — and it is doubtful whether DE POINCY refers to Greenland at all, while the Museum Regium is only one of the many contemporary Museum Catalogues in which objects from Greenland are included[1] — are, with the exception of the two well-known works of MARTIN FROBISHER and JOHN DAVIS, all that the Editor gives us regarding the land east of Davis Straits. It is thus but a very scanty and casual selection; he cannot be said to have mastered his subject to the full[2].

Small as it is, however, this selection, and the manner in which it has been treated will yet suffice to convince the reader that the short-comings of the work as a whole can at any rate not be laid to the charge of the National Museum, since the same faults are apparent in the sections compiled by Mr. THALBITZER from library and home studies.

What we have seen in the foregoing with regard to the Author's manner of dealing with his subject matter warrants a certain doubt as to the results which may be arrived at by such methods. This element of doubt is further increased by a closer study of the work.

To examine thoroughly, point by point, the whole of this loosely written and not particularly readable book would prove wearying alike to the critic and his readers, the more so, since the Author's own conclusions regarding one and the same object vary at different parts of the work. We must restrict ourselves to such brief consideration of certain portions as may serve in some degree to guide those wishing to make use of the book as a whole.

CONTRIBUTION TO THE HISTORY OF ANGMAGSALIK.

The earliest printed report in which the name Angmagsalik is mentioned dates from the visit of certain East Greenlanders to the nearest Danish trading outpost Pamiagdluk, in 1860[3]. The earliest mention of the place by name is, however, somewhat prior to this, viz. 1849, when the first objects were brought home from there.

These objects, a water vessel and dipper[4] were sent to the then Ethnographical Museum by Kolonibestyrer O. V. KIELSEN, with the following information: "These two objects, the like of which no Greenlander

---

[1] E. g. Museum Wormianum, Gottorfische Kunstkammer etc. etc.
[2] Any reader seeking a fuller selection may find the same in the Bibliographia Groenlandica" above quoted. (Medd. om Grønl. vol. 13.)
[3] H. RINK: Danish Greenland. London 1877, p. 322; cf. THALB. II, p. 340—41.
[4] Ethnographical collection of the National Museum. Nos L. c. 267—68.

had ever seen, were brought to Julianehaab by a family from Angmar-selik, a place on the East Coast, said to be situated considerably farther to the north than Captain GRAAH's farthest point". These two objects, which are of interest as being the first ever brought home from Ang-magsalik, are shown in W. THALBITZER's work as Fig. 280c and 273, both being there attributed, however, to the HOLM collection.

The water tub (Fig. 280c) is, it is true, larger than the other vessels from the same locality preserved in the Museum, but is in the main of the same shape as these. The dipper, however, (Fig. 273) merits closer consideration, being an interesting item in itself, though its peculiarity will hardly be realised at once from Mr. THALBITZER's description.

It is a bottle-shaped vessel, carved out of a lump of wood, but with a separate bottom nailed on. The Editor describes it thus: "Besides the drinking hole at the top of the neck there is a hole in the middle of the side so that it can be half filled without being put quite down into the water. This is very practical as the water-vessel is not always quite filled, and it may be difficult owing to the melting pieces of ice in it to let down the scoop or the bottle deep enough[1]".

The extremely practical nature of this arrangement is less obvious when it is added, that the bottle is also furnished with a hole on the opposite side, this last hole being bored some 5 cm. only above the bot-tom. A thirsty man, attempting to drink from such a bottle, would hardly appreciate the value of the holes, through one or other of which the water would infallibly be spilt. From his photograph of the object, Cand. THALBITZER would of course only have been able to see one of these holes, and he had by that time evidently forgotten what he could hardly have failed to see when holding the object in his hand for actual inspection.

The Editor further says: "In JOHAN PETERSEN's collection there were also a few water-scoops and mugs of the same peculiar forms (Mikee-ki's water-scoop etc., Nos 213—216)" The expression "Mikeeki's water-scoop etc." is incomprehensible to the uninitiated, referring as it does to the unpublished catalogue of a private collection which the Editor was at that time endeavouring to dispose of abroad"[2]. The collec-tion has, however, since passed into the possession of the National Museum, so that we are in a position to explain the Editor's mea-ning. No. 213 is, it is true, of the same type, the others, however,

---

[1] THALB. II, p. 548.

[2] The value of this collection could hardly have been unknown to the Editor, since he mentions the name of the collector on the title-page of his work, and gives illustrations of over 50 of the objects included. The owner of the collection, however, could not be aware of its importance to the Danish Museum; had he been so we may be sure, from his former services ren-dered to the Museum, that he would first have offered the objects in question to his own country.

214—16, are of a different although in itself typical form, which fact the Editor has not seen fit to note (Fig. 1 in the present work)[1].

From the dipper No. 213 the Editor might have gained some idea as to the purpose of the two holes in the ancient bottle from 1849. They were intended, as a matter of fact, to receive a wooden tube, the lower end of which fitted into the lower and smaller of the two holes, the tube itself serving both as a handle and a sucking pipe. Its length was such as to permit of the bottle being entirely filled, the air passing out through the tube while the vessel was filling. This Eskimo drinking vessel certainly seems to reveal a higher degree of ingenuity than the Tantalus arrangement suggested by Mr. THALBITZER's explanation. The fact of this bottle's having originally been furnished with a sucking pipe of this nature is noted, by the way, in the Museum Register.

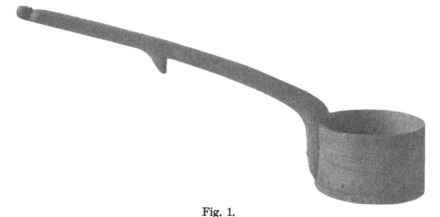

Fig. 1.

In view of the interest attaching to this old-fashioned article, I approached Kolonibestyrer JOHAN PETERSEN with the object of gaining some further information as to his specimen. He informed me that it had been made to order especially for his collection, on the model of a type then obsolete. This fact is also noted in the Museum Register.

Mr. THALBITZER concludes his remarks with the following words: "These objects (the wooden bottle etc.) show us some recent examples of the Ammassalikers' skill in converting pieces of material of different shapes — here a round piece of wood — into useful objects which are not typical, rather quite unique, but may however, serve for practical purposes". It should be observed, however, as we have seen from the foregoing, in the first place, that the objects are not "recent examples" of Angmagsalik work one of them being the oldest piece of work ever brought home from there, and further, that they are, according to JOHAN PETERSEN's explanation, old and typical forms.

---

[1] The name Mikeeki, however, does not occur anywhere in the English catalogue of the collection lodged in the Museum.

WHETTING IRONS.

Besides whetstones, iron is now also used at Angmagsalik for whetting knives. Kolonibestyrer Johan Petersen states, according to W. Thalbitzer, that the iron is only used for sharpening women's knives, whereas the men still whet their knives on stone. Thus the women in this case stand for progress, since the whetting iron cannot be of very ancient date in a place where iron was so rare that pieces were often hacked off from the women's knives to make needles. Some specimens are, however, preserved in the National Museum, three of them shown in W. Thalbitzer's work.

Two characteristic examples are shown in Fig. 190: "Drills or whetting irons? (Holm coll.)" and are mentioned on pp. 479—80 under drills, as follows: "The two, very finely worked wooden hafts (drills?) in fig. 190, which were likewise[1] brought home by Holm from Ammassalik, have regular ring grooves either for ornament or as bed for the drill line. The one has a thin cylindrical iron point, the other a heavier point, square in section (cf. fig. 202) with blunt end. The form of the shafts of these sticks is extremely rare even at Ammassalik, but incisions carved in the shaft to keep the string in position are known from other Eskimo regions (Baffin Land and Alaska)". And in a footnote, the Editor refers to "Boas (1901) p. 28; see figs. 36 and 37b, c. Murdoch (1892) fig. 159".

It is thus evident that the Author entertains some doubt as regards these objects, more especially in connection with the grooves in the hafts; he reassures his readers, however, by reference to competent authorities. One is therefore somewhat surprised to find, a little farther on, the following remarks anent whetstones: "The two drill-like objects in fig. 190 are (according to Johan Petersen) whetting irons for women's knives whereas men's knives are always sharpened on whetstones".

In the face of this, we must,. it seems, relinquish altogether the "drill" alternative, and accept, once and for all, the two formerly doubtful implements brought back by Holm as whetting irons. On the last page of the book, however, (p. 755) we find the term "whetting irons" again qualified by a parenthetic query "(drills?)" in addition to which, the implements in question are here included among the objects concerning which the Editor is in doubt as to whether they may possibly have originated from Graah's voyage, or have been sent over later by Johan Petersen.

Despite Johan Petersen's negation, the Editor is still, as we see, loth to relinquish his original idea: we can only suppose that he must have some strong grounds for retaining it.

Such grounds would hardly be furnished by the appearance of the objects themselves, which exhibit but very slight resemblance to drills. To the description given should, by the way, be added that the hafts are over 2 cm. thick at the top, the one marked b. being perfectly flat

---

[1] This refers to Fig. 191 of which, however, c. was brought home by Ryder.

at the end, so that they are hardly suitable for use with the mouthpiece. As regards the points, it should be noted that neither of them is sharp, the "point" of a., for instance, being a flat surface 8 mm square. With regard to the reference to Fig. 202, however, as a drill "used for making large holes" it should be noted that this implement is pointed.

It would seem then, that the Editor's opinion as regards the purpose of these implements must rest on the fact of similar instruments being found among other Eskimos. We may therefore proceed to consult the authorities he quotes.

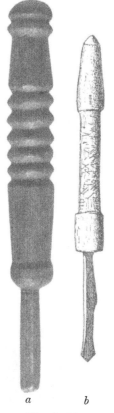

Boas' Fig. 36 does not include a drill haft at all. What Cand. THALBITZER has taken for a shaft is, as a matter of fact, the drill bow itself. The text on p. 28 simply states: "The shaft of the drill is always thin in the middle, to prevent the strap of the bow from sliding off (Fig. 37)". Figs. 37b and c, and MURDOCH Fig. 159 again, illustrate nothing more than just this very feature. For greater convenience of comparison, one of the two whetting irons in question is shown in Fig. 2a of the present work, together with the most characteristic of the drill shafts given in the illustrations quoted.

The Editor need not, by the way, have remained long in doubt either as to the origin of the implements concerned or as to their purpose; full information on both heads could have been obtained on enquiry at the Museum; HOLM has expressly noted them, at time of delivery, as whetting irons[1].

Another of HOLM's whetting irons, a peculiar piece of work, is shown in THALBITZER's Fig. 218c together with two other objects, together described there as "whetting stones". That the term is not due to a printer's error may be seen from the text, where we are informed that "the stone" is "inserted in a wooden haft carved like a dog (?)".

a　　　　*b*

Fig. 2. $^1/_2$.
(*b* After F. BOAS: Eskimo of Baffin Land and Hudson Bay fig. 37c).

The Editor might well be unable to see from his photograph, that the "stone" was of iron, he must, however, when actually handling it in the Museum, have given the object but slight scrutiny. Nevertheless, Museum studies apart, he might easily have ascertained the true facts of the case from the book; the piece in question is shown in one of the illustrations in the Danish edition of HOLM's work[2] together with a number of women's knives, and there described as "a whetting iron for

[1] They are two of the four described as "4 whetting irons" in the catalogue of the collection as given in Medd. om Grønland, vol 10, p. 353.

[2] Medd. om Grønland, 10.　Plate XIX h.

sharpening knives". He might even have read, what he himself had written, in his own English edition of the same work, the following passage: "A whetting iron inserted in a handle of wood is used for grinding knives with (fig. 218c)"[1] — referring, it will be noted, to this very figure.

These two instances, then, the water vessel and the whetting irons, serve to confirm the truth of the Editor's own very apt remark, which might well be taken as a motto for any ethnographical work based on museum studies: "It is a good thing to have a photograph of an ethnographic object, but still better to study it in the hand, view it from all sides, and possibly make a sketch of it[2]".

IRON-BLADED CHISEL.

The whetting iron is ethnologically interesting as representing a certain type of implement; the importance of various iron tools occasionally found, on the other hand, lies in the fact of their illustrating the manner in which odd scraps of iron accidentally acquired are utilised by the finder to serve his own particular needs.

A specimen of such more occasional implements is the little iron chisel, fastened to a handle by thongs, which is shown in THALBITZER'S Fig. 189, but there erroneously described as a hammer.

The illustration in itself should suffice to show the inaccuracy of this. The position in which the blade is fixed to the handle alone renders it impossible. The tool might with more excuse have been described as an axe. The blade is, however, quite small and light, with a distinct chisel edge at the one end, and evident marks of having been driven by a hammer at the other. All this might have been discovered by mere observation.

Here again, however, other sources of information were likewise open to the Author had he cared to use them. The tool in question is, in the first place, like the whetting iron just mentioned, shown in an illustration of that very work of which Mr. THALBITZER's book is a new and improved edition, and is there described as a chisel[3]. And in the second place, Mr. THALBITZER would, as a linguist, have had excellent opportunities of discovering, by actual inquiry among the Eskimo themselves, what was the true purpose of the implement. As to this, he remarks, on p. 678: "The word ilageen which I have erroneously given for a hammer like that seen in Fig. 189 means ,a wedge for splitting wood', possibly also a celt, a chisel". And we are further told: "The Eskimo, who was shown the illustration of a hammer in HOLM's book, evidently considered

---

[1] Thalb. II, p. 35.

[2] Thalb. II, p. 327.

[3] Medd. om Grønland, vol. 10. Plate XVIIIg.

the head as a wedge or a celt, and told me its name, which I then erroneously took to be the name of the hammer as a whole".

It should be noted, that the illustration in Holm's book shown to the Eskimo was the very one here in question; the Eskimo then at once gave the thing its right name, which was the same as that appended to the illustration by Holm himself. This was an excellent test of the Eskimo intelligence; unfortunately, however, Mr. Thalbitzer declined to be guided thereby.

It may be as well in this connection to call to mind the reasons which persuaded Cand. Thalbitzer in 1906 to publish the description of the Amdrup collection. After declaring that the work lay "outside of the special line of study" which he "had hitherto pursued", he goes on to mention, among the objects which induced him to undertake it, the following: "in my capacity of linguist I was sensible of the advantage of obtaining a better insight into the forms assumed by the material culture of the East Greenlanders".... and concludes: "An exact knowledge of the objects and their modifications will always come in useful in studying a people's linguistic designations of these objects"[1].

The last sentence is confirmed by the case of the chisel just referred to. The linguist may easily be misled if he does not happen to know the Danish name of the object which he wishes to have named in the Eskimo tongue.

AN ESKIMO WORK OF ART.

Among the finest pieces of work in Johan Petersen's collection is a little double head, carved in wood (Thalbitzer's Fig. 356). The one face shows, in a very realistic manner, the typical Eskimo features, while the other reveals the large nose and numerous wrinkles typical of the masks from East Greenland.

The Editor states that the object was found "in a grave in the Ammassalik Fjord" and expresses the opinion that "it may probably have been a memorial image like those known from Alaska (Nelson 1899 pp. 317—319)[2] belonging to a grave and representing the deceased sealer and his wife".

With regard to the reference made to Nelson's work, it should be noted that the objects described by him on the pages quoted are either large figures (the measurements given say 6—7 feet high, whereas the present head is only 11 cm.) or large flat masks, placed side by side on a palisade. The placing of such figures is, moreover, not an ordinary burial custom, but is confined to memorials erected over persons who had met their death elsewhere, and were thus precluded from receiving the usual funeral rites.

[1] Medd. om Grønl. vol. 28 p. 334. [2] Ann. Rep. of the Bur. of Am. Ethnol. XVIII.

If then, the object in question had been found in a grave, the reference to NELSON's work would not apply. It was therefore thought desirable to look up JOHAN PETERSEN's own catalogue of the collection, and see if perchance the object might have been found beside a grave. The list in question, has, however, neither the one nor the other, but states simply: "Carved head or double mask found by excavation (Udgravning) of an old house in the Angmagsalik Fjord".

In view of the new light thus cast upon the origin of this figure, it will doubtless be best to leave the Editor's theory alone, and content ourselves with appreciating the object itself, as the finest piece of picture work hitherto produced by East Greenland Eskimos.

WODDEN DOLLS.

A very considerable number of dolls, differing greatly as to size and manner of execution, have in course of time found their way to the National Museum; as a matter of fact they may be counted in hundreds. It is therefore but natural, that in a work like Cand. THALBITZER's, they should be accorded a chapter to themselves.

With regard to this section there is a good deal to be said.

Fig. 366, for instance, shows a number of small figures there described as "Dolls carved in wood". Here again, however, it must be observed, albeit at the risk of wearying the reader with repetition, that the Editor's eye has been at fault with regard to the material: the dolls marked l. and m. are carved in bone, and are identical with the two shown in Plate XXVIII (left upper corner) in HOLM's original edition, and in THALBITZER's illustration on p. 115 of his English edition of the same work.

The Author commences by observing that the dolls "must be considered in the main as toys but it is possible, that by the grown-up people they were formerly given a significance beyond their capacity as playthings". And in support of this suggestion he quotes "RYDER (1895) pp. 139—140; GRAAH (1832) p. 101".

The reader, wishing to consult the former of these two writers, may look up the List of works consulted. He will there find: "C. RYDER: Om den tidligere eskimoiske Bebyggelse af Scoresby Sound. M. o. Grønland, vol. 17, Kbhvn. 1895". RYDER's work on the subject referred to commences, however, on p. 281; but the same volume of the Medd. om Grønland contains another work of RYDER's, not quoted by the Editor, viz: "Beretning om den østgrønlandske Expedition 1891—92," in which we read, on p. 139—40:

> Justitsraad Steinhauer supposed that there was some higher religious significance attaching to the wooden small figures or dolls

brought home by Captain Holm in considerable numbers, (Medd. om Grønland vol. 10, Plate XXVII) as also to the entirely similar ones found on the West Coast during excavation of old Greenlandic graves and sites of houses. True, the natives of Angmagsalik are wont to use, *inter alia*, male and female figures as amulets, which are sewn into the amulet straps worn by the men, or fixed in the hair-knot or fur worn by the women (Medd. om Grønl. vol. 10, p. 118), such figures being also, albeit in highly conventionalised form, utilised for the decoration of sewing-needle skins (Medd. om Grønl. vol. 10. Pl. XXVIII) and for ornamenting various implements, in which cases there is doubtless some fundamental idea as to the figures' affording some protection or advantage to the owner. Such figures are, however, of an entirely different character to the wooden dolls first mentioned[1]), which are generally executed with greater attention to detail and as a rule considerably larger than the amulets, the latter bearing but a suggestion of the human form. The wooden dolls are now used by the natives of Angmagsalik only as toys for children, and both Captain Holm's expedition and we ourselves procured numbers of them by barter, every child having as a rule a little collection. Another feature which further shows that no higher significance is attached to them is the fact that the natives show not the slightest unwillingness to part with them, whereas they are very loth, and in most cases absolutely refuse, to give up their amulets, even for a considerable price. In addition to the dolls carved in human form, the children often had figures of animals carved in wood, representing bears, foxes, dogs and seals. The wooden dolls were always kept together with these figures and the other playthings, and were treated in the same way, the whole stock being sometimes tied together with a strip of sealhide. From this it would seem that the wooden dolls are nothing but playthings"[1].

And to avoid any possibility of misunderstanding, RYDER further adds:

"The fact of dolls having been found in graves on the West coast proves nothing, it being a general custom among the Eskimos to place in the grave some articles belonging to the deceased"[1].

It is difficult to understand how these words can be taken as evidence in support of the theory as to a former religious significance attaching to the dolls: we are therefore obliged to have recourse to the other writer quoted, viz: GRAAH. He writes, with regard to some houses and graves on Snedorffs Island, as follows: "In these there lay, together with the usual hunting implements, two human images carved in wood, not unlike those presented to Bering by the savages on the N.W. coast of Ame-

---

[1] Spaced type by THOMAS THOMSEN.

rica, and which he took to be idols; it is probable, however, that they were not considered on that coast as more or less than in Greenland, where such dolls are only playthings for children"[1].

This method of quoting — and we have previously encountered some instances of the same thing in the foregoing — renders the book somewhat difficult to read with advantage, as it involves the necessity of having the sources quoted at hand, which, in the case of unpublished works, is for readers abroad an impossibility.

It is not unusual, when at a loss for an explanation, to have recourse to the religious idea; the Author has, however (p. 647) here employed this expedient in such a manner as to preclude all reasonable discussion. "Fig. 368a is a fairly large doll evidently representing a woman in the sitting position without hair top, arms and nose but with nostrils and inlaid eyes in the orbits; the mouth is distended like the mouth of a person playing *uaajeertoq* and dark with blood. The doll probably represents some supernatural being and must be considered as male".

Something more in the way of explanation might well have been vouchsafed this remarkable figure. The next one, on the other hand, a perfectly new jointed doll (Fig. 368b) receives an unmerited share of attention. On p. 647 we read: "Is this doll possibly a variety of East Greenland origin? Among the Eskimo living outside Greenland this kind of doll has not been found so far as I know". The last sentence is however, not to be taken as disposing of the question raised, for in a note on p. 681 we find the subject taken up for discussion anew, in the Addenda, included between the descriptive portion and the results. We read here: "Wooden dolls with pliable joints in arms and legs have been mentioned from the Chukchee and Koryaks in north-eastern Asia. There is reason consequently to believe that the same kind of dolls found among the Ammassalikers is an Eskimo product of old origin".

I cannot concur in this view, but should nevertheless be loth to devote further space to the subject were it not that Mr. THALBITZER himself attaches so great importance to it: "This — like many other facts of a similar kind mentioned by me — shows how cautious we must be in considering the apparently surprising agreement with modern objects from our own shops as due to 'European influence'[2]. We have probably here another proof that the Ammassalikers like all other East Greenlanders have stuck tenaciously in their isolation to certain old forms of implements, cult and luxury long after the same things have

---

[1] Spaced type by THOMAS THOMSEN.
[2] The words "European influence" are set in inverted commas by Mr. THALBITZER himself, presumably indicating his extreme contempt for such a view.

disappeared from the west coast and even from among the western kinsmen on the opposite side of the Davis Straits".

Why stop at the Koryaks? By a second spring like the first he would reach Greece, and dolls with movable joints were known there, as we are aware, in ancient times. Yet perhaps, after all, it would be better to keep a little closer to the dolls of Greenland. There are over 170 of these from Angmagsalik in the Museum. Of these one only, to wit, that brought back by THALBITZER himself in 1906, which is quite new, has four pairs of movable joints. Seven others, likewise apparently new, are jointed at the knees, to make them "sit down"; all the others are perfectly rigid. Turning to Western Greenland, we find that not one out of some sixty dolls found in old villages and graves has movable joints; such are, however, found in a few figures of recent date, viz. a group of bone figures representing a drum dance[1], and another group of four dogs in a team.

It seems thus more natural to suggest "European influence", either as coming direct from Denmark, which is undoubtedly the case with the jointed doll in question, or indirectly by way of the West Coast. It should be borne in mind that the frequently mentioned isolation of Angmagsalik is not to be taken too literally, or rather, that it is of recent date, and artificially created, the foundation of the Danish trading station having prevented the natives there from following their fellows on the southern side of the station down to the colonies of the West Coast. It was not until the close of the last, and beginning of the present century that the southern portion of the East Coast was entirely forsaken, and the isolation rendered complete. During the last century, the products of the West Coast could still find their way up along the East, and much may have reached Angmagsalik in this way.

Mr. THALBITZER himself, by the way, is in other parts of his work not disposed to reject altogether the idea of such influence. He considers, for instance, that the wooden objects shown in Fig. 241 are imitations of an almanack such as that shown in Fig. 392. In this particular instance, however, I am loth to accept the imitation theory, as the resemblance is not very great. The almanack has one hole for each day of the week; of Mr. THALBITZER's specimens the one has 9 holes of different sizes, the other 23, — of which, however, 7 in the middle line — in addition to which, no such almanack has been shown to have originated from Angmagsalik, the object in question being, as we have seen, from a more southerly part of the East Coast.

As regards the Koryak dolls, by the way, the appearance of these is but vaguely described in the passage quoted from JOCHELSON (THALB. p. 681, Note 2) and no illustration is given. Mr. THALBITZER, moreover, in the same note, compares these with a toy bear from East Greenland

---

[1] Labels of the National Museum: East Greenland No. 57.

in the AMDRUP collection. I do not know whether he bases this comparison on personal acquaintance with JOCHELSON's dolls; if so, then they are not made with movable joints, for the bear in question has no movable joints, its legs being merely pegged into their sockets (*vide* THALB. I, p. 534, Fig. 105).

SHARK'S TOOTH KNIVES AND UMIAK CLEANERS.

With regard to the strange knives edged with shark's teeth, Mr. THALBITZER observes[1]: "Shark's tooth knives (Fig. 187) for cutting hair have been mentioned[2] on p. 32. Such knives seem also to have been known in West Greenland in earlier times, for OLEARIUS mentions, that his Greenlanders had some knives, which they called *ekalugsaa*, that is they explained with this word, that the knives were made from sharks (presumably the teeth of sharks)[6]). The teeth are inserted into grooves along both edges, like the small iron blades in the primitive knives we know from northern West Greenland and Southampton Island (see p. 489)". Note 6 runs as follows: "OLEARIUS (1656), p. 174. Illustration from southern East Greenland by GRAAH (1832) Pl. VII".

Glancing first at Fig. 187, we here find two knives shown, and stated by the Author as belonging to the HOLM collection. This is true, however, only as regards 187a, that marked b. being as a matter of fact the very one brought home by GRAAH and mentioned by Mr. THALBITZER in Note 6 as from southern East Greenland (to be precise, from Malingisek, Lat. 62°20′N.); it should be noted, however, that the knife will be found shown in GRAAH's book, not in Pl. VII, but in Pl. VIII.

The reference to OLEARIUS is, like Mr. THALBITZER's earlier quotation of the same author[3], not altogether correct. OLEARIUS says, in the passage in question, "Ihre Messer seind von Backen Zähnen eines Meerfisches, welchen sie Ekulugsua, Piso aber in historia naturali Brasiliæ p. 180 und Jonstonius de piscib. p. 201 Piratia Pua auf Brasilianisch nennen".

The form "welchen" must necessarily refer to "Meerfisch" and not, as Mr. THALBITZER's seems to have read, to "Ihre Messer". Properly construed, the words of OLEARIUS tell us, clearly and distinctly enough, that it is the fish, not the knife, which the Greenlanders called Ekulugsua. He writes the work ekulugsua, not, as Mr. THALBITZER spells it, ekalugsaa, and intends thereby to give the native name for the Greenland Shark (ekalugssuak). Nor is it easy to understand why the Editor, if he had read the passage in OLEARIUS, should find it necessary to advance the

---

[1] THALB. II, p. 476.
[2] i. e. by HOLM.
[3] vide supra p. 389 ff.

laboriously worded explanation: "that is they explained with this word, that the knives were made from sharks (presumably the teeth of sharks)" since OLEARIUS expressly states that they were made of "Backen Zähnen".

With regard to the closing words of the description: "The teeth are inserted into grooves along both edges, like the small iron blades in the primitive knives we know from northern West Greenland and Southampton Island (see p. 489)" it should be noted, 1) that shark's tooth knives may be single-edged, and 2) that the knives from Southampton Island are made, not with iron blades, but with stone[1], as Mr. THALBITZER himself, moreover, correctly states in the passage (p. 489) to which he refers.

We need not, by the way, hark back as far as the 17th century in order to find mention of shark's tooth knives from West Greenland. In 1872, JAPETUS STEENSTRUP, in his treatise "Sur l'emploi du fer meteorique par les Esquimaux du Groenland"[2] gave an illustration of a fragment of a shark's tooth knife, found in a grave in North Greenland. GRAAH's statement: "This instrument is also said to have been used in former times on the West Coast"[3] is of less weight, and may possibly be based on his recollections of OLEARIUS.

On p. 677, Mr. THALBITZER again reverts — as he frequently does in the case of other subjects dealt with — to the shark's tooth knives, and observes: "In the British Museum I have seen knives of a similar kind but much longer from the Hawaiian Islands, Polynesia, designated as ‚fighting weapons armed with shark's teeth'". Once more, it was not necessary to go so far afield; the National Museum in Copenhagen contains a whole series of similar large shark's tooth weapons from the Gilbert Islands. And in any case, it is not easy to see how the remark bears upon the point in question. It merely tells us, as most ethnographers already know, that sharks' teeth are used for making sharp instruments in some parts of the South Sea Islands. And the Editor admits that the objects to which he refers are not tools, but weapons, and differ considerably in point of size from the Greenland implements. It might further be added that the edge also is different in the two cases, the South Sea Islanders using single teeth, whereas in Greenland a whole row of teeth, still imbedded in the jaw, is used. Nevertheless, since Mr. THALBITZER inserts the remark in a special note, it must be presumed that he considers it of some relevant importance, and finds some connection between the small Greenland knives, edged with rows of teeth, and the large Hawaiian weapons in which single teeth are

---

[1] FRANZ BOAS: The Eskimo of Baffin Land and Hudson Bay (Bulletin of the American Museum of Natural History vol. XV) p. 384; Fig. 178, "Bone knives with stone blades".

[2] Compte rendu du congres international d'anthropologie et d'archéologie prehistoriques, 6me session, Bruxelles 1872, Pl. 25, fig. 1; cf. p. 248.

[3] Undersøgelsesrejse til Østkysten af Grønland. Kbh. 1832, p. 85.

used, albeit Hawaii lies some 45° farther south and 100° to the west, no intermediate station being named.

The Author makes frequent use of comparative methods. An instance of this we have already seen in the case of the dolls[1], and another is furnished by the Editor's treatment of the umiak cleaner[2]. The object in question is an implement some 30 cm. long, consisting of a bear's claw fixed to a haft; we know for a certainty that it is used for cleaning umiaks[3], and that is all we do know. Nevertheless the following remarks are added: "It is not improbable, that this instrument is useful in certain cases for more than simply cleaning the boat. Turner mentions "boat-hooks" as belonging to the complete outfit of a kayak among the Eskimo of Hudson Bay, used for all purposes of a boat hook and also to retrieve a sunken animal' (seal). It is possible that the Ammassalikers' umiak cleaner is a transformed relict of this instrument".

There does not seem, on the face of it, to be any very great probability that this little tool, used for cleaning, and belonging to the umiak, should be a relict of a boat hook appertaining to the kayak. And TURNER's description does not incline one the more towards Mr. THALBITZER's opinion.

TURNER begins by stating the length as about 8 feet, whereupon he describes the implement as follows: "The lower end of this has a strong hook made of stout iron set into it. Along the inner edge of the wooden shaft two or three notches are cut. The end near the person has a V-shaped notch cut into it .... A weight is attached to near the hook end to keep the shaft perpendicular in the water. A line of sufficient length is attached to it".

Clearly, the implement has in process of transformation, apart from shrinking to an eight of its former size, and being relegated from the kayak to the umiak, lost not a few of its originally characteristic features. A series of intermediate stages, showing the transition, not only in form, but also in purpose, would not be out of place.

True, Mr. THALBITZER here expresses himself but cautiously; "it is possible" "it is not improbable", yet the manner in which the term "boat hooks" is placed as an alternative designation at the outset — the heading runs: "Umiak cleaners (p. 43, cf. fig. 83) — or boat-hooks?" — gives the effect of something more than a casual suggestion, and the Author's belief in his hypothesis increases as the work goes on; thus on p. 728 we find, among the implements or forms of same peculiar to Angmag-

---

[1] vide supra pp. 402—403.
[2] THALB. II, p. 380, fig. 83. The reader will doubtless not be surprised to learn that not both of the umiak cleaners shown in fig. 83 belong to the HOLM collection. 83a was brought over by Mr. THALBITZER himself in 1906.
[3] HOLM (Medd. om Grønland, vol. 10). Pl. XXVI, fig. b; cf. the text.

salik, "boat hooks („umiak cleaners')". It will be noticed that the term "boat-hook" is here accorded the principal place, while "umiak cleaner" is packed away in a parenthesis with inverted commas.

HARPOONS.

With regard to the East Greenland kayak harpoon, Mr. THALBITZER writes, on p. 411:

"I may refer to G. HOLM's description here p. 46 and to O. MASON's detailed description, which like his other studies on the Aboriginal American Harpoons, is very instructive.

On only one point in MASON's account is a correction necessary. In his description of the East Greenland harpoon he states: „The fore-shaft[1] is in this specimen a cap of ivory, squared off on top, and the middle left projecting for the socket on the base of the loose shaft'[2] (l. c., p. 238)[3]. According to this the loose shaft would have ,a socket on the basal surface, covering a corresponding projection on the top of the foreshaft. The same explanation is repeated in describing a second example from South Greenland- and his illustration of this part of the harpoon (fig. 49 in MASON) shows the same peculiar feature. It is probably based on some mistake. The condition in all the Greenland harpoons, which I have seen, has always been that the tenon (or projection) was on the base of the loose shaft and the socket on the flat top of the foreshaft. There is some doubt, as to whether MASON has described his own specimens correctly on this point. In the first place it is unusual, that the two Greenland harpoons, he describes, should differ from the Greenland type known elsewhere; in the second place, there is a contradiction in MASON's description. On the same page, namely, where he describes the foreshaft erroneously (p. 238) he explains, in full agreement with the usual type of Greenland harpoon, that the loose shaft has a ,flat surface at the base, with a projection in the middle, fitting into a cavity on the front of the foreshaft' and his drawing of this harpoon (Pl. 4) is accurate and correct. It thus appears, that through forgetfulness he has given an erroneous description of the ball-and-socket joint which he had described correctly on referring to the loose shaft".

And in a note, we read: "In F. NANSEN's "Eskimoliv" (1891) p. 31 there is a drawing of the front end of a harpoon, which, though indistinctly, shows the same error in confusing the loose shaft and foreshaft. NANSEN is cited by MASON (l. c. p. 240)".

---

[1] By this MASON understands the bone part in the fore-end of the harpoon shaft.

[2] By loose shaft is meant the piece of bone between the shaft and the head.

[3] O. T. MASON: Aboriginal American Harpoons. Washington 1902.

For convenience of comparison, MASON's two illustrations are here shown in Fig. 3—4.

The Editor is right in saying, that MASON, after giving a perfectly correct description of the loose shaft, and describing — likewise correctly

— the foreshaft in this specimen as having a projection, incorrectly adds: "for the socket on the base of the loose shaft". Even the uninitiated reader will at once see from the illustration that the description is incorrect only in this one point (Fig. 3).

Had Mr. THALBITZER stopped at this, all would have been well. Not content however, with challenging the description of the East Greenland harpoon, he goes so far as to include the South Greenland also (Fig. 4). In this case, however, MASON's description will be found to be in entire agreement with his illustration, which suggests the possibility of Mr. THALBITZER's having misunderstood the passage, the more so, since we are told that FRIDTJOF NANSEN gives a drawing "which, though indistinctly, shows the same error in confusing the loose shaft and the foreshaft".

Fig. 3.
(After O. T. MASON: Aboriginal American Harpoons pl. 4).

Might it not now be worth while to look closer into the matter, and see if possibly Mr. THALBITZER himself may be in error? It will soon be realised that the main point lies in the sentence about the two Greenland harpoons which are said to "differ from the Greenland type known elsewhere". "The Greenland type as known to the Editor" would have been more correct. As a matter of fact, Fig. 3 is from East Greenland, whereas Fig. 4 is from the southern part of West Greenland, NANSEN's specimen being presumably from the Godthaab district.

Mr. THALBITZER declares that all the Greenland harpoons he has seen have always had "the tenon (or projection) .... on the base of the loose shaft and the socket on the flat top of the foreshaft".

Fig. 4.
(After O. T. MASON: Aboriginal American Harpoons fig. 49).

Strange, that with all his journeyings in search of information, — to Berlin (1904, 1907 and 1912) to Vienna (1908) to Christiania (1908) to Stockholm (1908 and 1910), London (1909) and Dublin (1909)[1] he should never have come across harpoons of the other type. I do not know what the Museums of these cities may have to show in this respect; I can, however, refer Mr. THALBITZER to the series of 10 harpoons and 6

---

[1] THALB. II, p. 328.

lances preserved in the West Greenland section of the National Museum at Copenhagen, which somehow appear to have escaped his attention[1].

A peculiar form of harpoon is used by sealers hunting in couples on the ice. This weapon is called by HOLM the Ituartit harpoon[2], which term was generally accepted until Cand. THALBITZER in 1909 chose to style it the "Ituartin" harpoon. Here obviously the linguist must be right, and those unversed in the Greenland tongue had perforce to recognise the new name. In 1914, however, with the publication of Mr. THALBITZER's work, complications arose. We here find, on p. 422, among "Technical names", the "ittuarteen, itcīarteen harpoon"; the Editor does not, however, restrict himself to these technical terms, but uses also "ituartit harpoon" (p. 409; p. 412), "ice sealing harpoon (ittuarteq)" (p. 421; p. 433) and "ittuartin" (p. 420). Disregarding the phonetic spelling, and overlooking the difference between one "t" and "tt" as immaterial, we have still four different terms remaining. That all four are current and correct we do not venture to doubt, since the linguist uses them indiscriminately, and we may rest assured that there is some valid linguistic reason for the fact that only two of them are included under the heading "technical names". The ordinary reader, however, not being a linguist, comes to a standstill here, with the obvious query: "What am I to call the thing?" I for my part have thought it safest for the present to keep to the term originally given by HOLM: "Ituartit".

In his paper published in 1909, Mr. THALBITZER haled forth from the Stockholm Museum a couple of ordinary West Greenland tow-line toggles, which he showed in illustration as points of ituartit harpoons[3]; in 1914, however, (p. 433) he makes reparation for the error in the following words: "The whole form of the weapons, however, makes this

---

[1] The young Danish ethnographer, KAI BIRKET SMITH, has already, in a lecture delivered to "Det Grønlandske Selskab" referred to this point as "one of the inaccuracies which have crept into the description of Kommandør HOLM's collection recently published by the linquist WILL. THALBITZER". Hr. BIRKET SMITH's studies in South Greenland, and among the collections in the National Museum, had shown him that Mr. THALBITZER was but imperfectly acquainted with the Greenland harpoon. He was also aware, moreover, that the East Greenland form was derived from the original type, whereas that shown in fig. 4 is a variant which later made its appearance on the West Coast. He did not, however, — as far as can be judged from the text of the lecture as published in Det grønlandske Selskabs Aarsskrift, 1912 — perceive that MASON's illustration of the East Greenland harpoon agreed with the form of all other East Greenland harpoons, and that it was only in his description that any inaccuracy existed. Since the above was written a correction has been made in the text of the lecture as published (Det Grønlandske Selskabs Aarsskrift, 1914, p. 62).

[2] Medd. om Grønland, vol. 10, p. 78 and THALB. II (i. e. HOLM) p. 51.

[3] THALB. I, p. 501.

explanation improbable" — which honest admission is in perfect accord with the fact.

But Mr. THALBITZER does not stop here. He goes on to say "it is curious to find a bone implement of precisely the same construction, a towing or drag toggle, which is also stated to be in the Stockholm Riksmuseum, namely in A. E. NORDENSKIÖLD's collection from Alaska, (the Vega Expedition)". Once again, we are led by the longest way to no advantage. The new result is based on a single specimen only, and the expression "stated to be" suggests that the Editor has not even seen this one himself. Had he cared to look through the West Greenland section of the National Museum, he would there have found a number of such "curiosities" whereby the error might have been avoided, and Mr. THALBITZER himself spared the necessity of making the new admission: "The hinged toggle has thus obtained here quite a different use from that we know in East Greenland, but the construction of the head is also of quite a different form".

The only point of similarity now remaining is thus the fact that in both cases two pieces of bone are joined together by means of a peg about which they can turn; this can, however, scarcely be regarded as a sufficient basis upon which to determine the class to which an implement belongs.

CONTENTS LISTS OF THE COLLECTIONS.

Pages 322—23 and 743—53 of the work are devoted to lists of the contents of some collections. The reader will naturally expect the collections in question to be those mentioned on the title-page of the book: as "Ethnographical collections from East Greenland, (Angmagsalik[1] and Nualik) made by G. HOLM, G. AMDRUP and J. PETERSEN and described by W. THALBITZER". This is, however not the case. Of the collection on which the whole work is based, to wit, HOLM's, no list is given; the Editor of this English work refers his readers to the Danish edition of HOLM's book, which according to the Editor's own statement, is out

---

[1] On the title-page of this section Mr. THALBITZER writes "Angmagsalik" according to KLEINSCHMIDT's orthography; on the page following, however, (p. 321, Note 1) he asserts that "the East Greenland form of this name is Ammattalik or Ammattaling". It might perhaps have been reasonable enough to have introduced one or other of these latter forms; it is less easy to realise, however, upon what grounds the Editor has, in the text of the work, supplanted the tradional form Angmagsalik by the term Ammassalik, which, according to the linguist himself, is the phonetic form of the word as used in the dialect of central West Greenland.

of print. Nor is there any catalogue of JOHAN PETERSEN's important collection. Of the three mentioned on the title-page, then, we find but one, viz. the AMDRUP collection, this being, however, accorded two lists: a brief classification on pp. 322—23, and another at greater length on pp. 743—52, both of which include, not only the objects from Angmagsalik and Nualik as stated on the title-page, but also the finds from the country farther to the north, which have already been treated by the Editor in his work of 1909, and of which an English catalogue already exists[1]. In lieu of the HOLM and JOH. PETERSEN collections, we are given a list of THALBITZER's collection.

The reader might, however, after all manage well enough without the missing lists, were it not that Mr. THALBITZER in the text of the work (p. 548) refers to some numbers in the one of them, for it must be admitted that catalogues reduced to such a degree of brevity as is evidenced by the following instances: "No. 36—38. Wooden plates and a spoon" or "No. 99—100 Sundry objects (plaited sinew threads etc.)[2]" can be of no value, and should certainly never have been included in a scientific work.

As regards the AMDRUP collection, we need here only concern ourselves with the lists of finds from the north, and will, for the sake of convenience, designate these as List I (THALB. I, 540—42), List II (THALB. II, 322—23) and List III (ibid. 743—52).

Far simpler would it have been had Lists II and III been given as reprints of List I, but in revised form, and with the corrections distinctly indicated. The three lists as they stand may easily give rise to doubt and misunderstanding.

List II may, on account of its extreme brevity, be disregarded; it is, however, in some respects preferable to List I, which includes only numbers up to 113, whereas the references in the text of the work go up to 121[3]. This incompleteness is corrected in List II, which brings the items from Cape Borlace Warren and Sabine Island up to No. 119, and even adds: "120—194 Finds from uncertain place north of Ammassalik". In List II we read "Skærgaards "Peninsula"", whereas I and III have "Skærgaardshalvø"; all three lists however, agree in stating the latitude of the place as 68°07', in contrast to the text, (THALB. I, p. 386) which gives it as 68°.

The uncertainty as to the size of the AMDRUP collection arising from the fact that List I gives numbers up to 113, Lists II and III up to 194, is further increased by an article of the Author's in Geographisk Tidsskrift[4], where the number is stated as over 300.

---

[1] THALB. I, pp. 540—42.
[2] THALB. II, pp. 752—53.
[3] THALB. I, pp. 495—99 and pp. 533—34.
[4] Geogr. Tidsskr. vol. XX, p. 215.

If we now proceed to compare Lists I and III, we find, in the figures alone, a series of other discrepancies calling for correction.

Inv. No.	List I	List III	
45	Fig. 21	Figs. 22	List I is here correct.
53	Fig. 26	Figs. 26 and 28	List III is here correct.
55—56	Fig. 29 a and b	Figs. 29 and 33	
86	Fig. 55	Figs. 55 and 561	should be: Figs. 55 and 56, p. 472 (No. 56 appearing twice in the same work).
87	Fig. 56	Fig. 562	Should be the second Fig 56, on p. 476.
90—95	Fig. 58	Figs. 58—60	List III is right,

two of the animals shown in Fig. 58 having turned out badly in the reproduction, wherefore they are shown again in Figs. 59—60. In Fig. 58, Mr. THALBITZER has altered the position of one of the animals, from the erect to the prone. The natural course in such a case would have been to remove the figure incorrectly reproduced, and replace it by the amended illustration; Mr. THALBITZER, however, has preferred to let the prone beast lie, and makes it the subject of the following passage:

"As all the animals just mentioned are rendered in a very lifelike manner in the carvings, there are no grounds for supposing that the sixth, *inv. AMD. 95*, should not also give a faithful representation of some animal or other. However it is by no means easy to identify it. It cannot be any kind of seal, as it has no swimmers, and the shape of the head with the small pointed ears is very unlike that of a seal. The imagination recoils from conceiving it as a land mammifer. And yet we have no other recourse, and we shall discover, to our surprise, that the realistic sense of the Eskimo has not failed him this time either. The drawing fig. 60 shows how the figure is to be conceived; not with the head in front and the tail behind, but with the head erected: a polar bear walking on its hind legs".

We may pass over the twenty further lines of print through which Mr. THALBITZER continues his explanation of the same figure, it should be observed, however, that the realistic execution of the object in question is not so great but that another scientific opinion pronounced it a hare. I leave the question open to the judgement of zoologists.

Turning now to discrepancies of another order, viz. in the classification of the objects themselves, we find, apart from minor differences of style, such instances as the following:

Inv. No.	List I	List III
31	Bodkin, or marline spike, of bone.	Bodkin-shaped wound plug of bone.
33—44	Bodkin and needles.	Bodkins.
55—56	Drum handles, 2, of bone.	Two handles of bone with finger-rests.
62	Wooden handle.	Handle-like object (cross piece of a bladder float?).
72	Wooden hammer-like implement (blubber-beater?)	Hammer-like implement (maul) made of a crooked branch.
80	Wooden handle of a skin-scraper.	Womans knife (scraper).
97	Fragment of a wooden implement.	Head of a wooden implement (fragment of a snow beater).
99	Shaft-like fragment of a wooden implement.	Handle part of a wooden implement (snow beater or blubber beater).
104—105	Miniature foreshafts of harpoons, 2.	Foreshaft like fragments (or toy harpoons?).

Such inconsistencies cannot but create a feeling of uncertainty in the mind of the reader. Have we here, as in the figures above referred to, but a series of errors due to negligence? Have the words "and needles" under 33—44 merely been omitted in List III? Or is the "wooden handle of a skin-scraper" a totally different object to the "woman's knife (scraper)" of List III, which must thus have crept in through some accidental error?

The answer to such queries is in the negative. The difference in terms is due to the change which the Author's opinion regarding one and the same object has undergone in course of time. An instance of this is furnished by Nos. 55—56. In his work of 1909, Mr. THALBITZER treats of these two objects, and comes to the result that they are drum handles, and further that they are the earliest finds of this type and material made in Greenland[1]. As to the features which the Editor here has regarded as of decisive importance, this may be seen from the following passage[2] referring to one of the specimens: "The drum-handle type, however, is unmistakable; we see the finger-rests and the remains of the knob-like head". These, however, would hardly appear to be the distinguishing marks of a drum handle, if we may judge from the difficulty which Mr. THALBITZER experiences in determining how the drum is fixed to the handle. After having devoted nine lines of print to the discussion of the question as to which end of the handle should be fixed to the frame of the drum, he concludes: "I feel convinced that it is the broad end of the handle which carried the drum, though I am not clear as to the mode in which it was secured"[3].

---

[1] THALB. I, pp. 412—17.
[2] THALB. I, p. 417.
[3] l. c., p. 416.

This last is not surprising, since the handles in question lack just that very notch into which the frame of the drum is inserted. The notches for the fingers merely prove that the object was intended as a handle of some kind or other, and the knob at the one end clearly indicates that the man who made it had here finished off his work in such a manner as to preclude the fastening of drum or any other instrument to that end at least.

By 1910, Mr. THALBITZER had realised the fact that this notch was lacking. In Geogr. Tidsskr. Vol. XX, p. 218, he tells us: "These hafts somewhat resemble drum handles, which are cut in the same manner in Alaska; both lack, however, it is true, the notch at the broad end into which the wooden ring of the drum is generally set and lashed, so that the explanation must be regarded as doubtful, unless supplementary finds should subsequently be made".

On p. 223 of the same work, we read "The two bone handles ... (presumably drum handles) .... are carved as if from the same model as a quiver handle shown by BOAS[1], from Vantissard Island". Here again however, it must be observed that the resemblance lies in the finger notching of the grip, the value of which as a distinctive feature of the drum handle generally is thus reduced, since they may equally well be taken as characteristic of quiver handles. Mr. THALBITZER has now discovered what is lacking in the two objects in question; he has not, however, as yet been able to see the distinctive attributes which they do possess, viz. a hole at the one end for the insertion of a blade, and an oblique boring at the other intended to receive a thong, two well known features in East Greenland knives.

In 1914 (THALB. II, p. 640, Note 5) we are brought somewhat nearer the truth: "They have possibly been knife-handles, not drum-handles". Thus from the "unmistakable drum-handles" of 1909 via doubtful drum-handle and quiver handle (both in the same paper 1910) we are at last, in 1914, brought within view of the actual fact; the Editor is careful, however, to leave a pathway open in case any new hypothesis should arise.

Without some kind of commentary, the reader will find serious difficulty in discovering what lies beneath such change of names, unless he happen to be particularly familiar with Mr. THALBITZER's published works, already of considerable extent. It may even at times be difficult enough to make List I agree with the accompanying text; it is not immediately obvious, for instance, that the object cited in List I as a "wooden hammer-like implement (blubber-beater?)" is identical with that treated in the text as forming part of the framework of an umiak. We cannot however, here undertake to guide the reader point by point through the

---

[1] Bulletin of the American Museum of Natural History, vol. XV, p. 420, fig. 219 e.

list. One or two other instances of metamorphosis will be mentioned later on; for the present, we may proceed to consider the catalogue of the second collection, viz. THALBITZER's.

When Cand. THALBITZER in 1909, on behalf of the Committee for the Investigation of Greenland, handed over the collection to the National Museum, it was accompanied by a catalogue drawn up and signed by the collector himself, marked "Copy" and dated Copenhagen 1907, with a further note: "Delivered to the National Museum 19 12 1909, W. T."

This list does not altogether agree with the one now published; it did not, by the way, altogether agree with the contents of the collection as delivered to the Museum. And in view of the fact that a published list, if allowed to pass without remark, might well be regarded as involving an obligation on the part of the Museum to produce the objects therein cited when called upon, it will be necessary to make some corrections.

List. No.

6—10. The two lists agree, but 6 specimens were received.

47—50. "Two masks carved of wood". There were three (L. 4853—55).

55—67. "Dolls dressed in skin clothes". These 13 numbers were noted in the list as "abt. 12" There were however 21 (L. 4858—77 and L. 4899).

71—88. "Various toys (nodding or pecking birds, puzzle with movable beads on a string, buzzes, ajagaq, tops, balls)". In the list delivered to the Museum these 18 numbers are represented by the following: Two toys (noqqataait) (L. 4912—13)[1] 2 ditto birds (L. 4909—10) 4 wing buzzes (imittitwaain).[2] One ajagaq game (L. 4911) — 3 tops (There were four: L. 4903—06). Three balls (L. 4916—18). One toy with two beads (puzzle) (L. 4945). Thus the published list gives 18 articles, the list delivered to the Museum 16, whereas the actual number received was 15. To these should be added, however, one object not noted on the list delivered, viz; a jumping animal (L. 4919) so that the Museum also received 16 pieces in all.

89—98. "Images of animals carved of wood or ivory". This lot is noted in the delivery list as "Various animals carved in wood" i. e. not in ivory. Fifteen of these were delivered to the Museum, not 10 as stated in the published list.

---

[1] Similar to that shown in Fig 876c as "bull roarer". The Eskimo name is not stated here, as in the case of the other toys, so that the List delivered to the Museum furnishes new information on this head.

[2] The original 2 in the list had been altered to a 4; there were, however, but two: L 4907—08.

99—100. "Sundry objects\ (plaited sinew threads etc.)". The sinew
thread is now marked No. L. 4947. The "etc." presumably
refers — although only one number is allotted — to various
small objects not noted in the list.

In addition, the list delivered also mentioned "One dust
cleaner" that is to say, an umiak cleaner, or as Mr. THAL-
BITZER prefers to call it, a boathook, this being the very
one shown in Fig. 83a p. 380 of Mr. THALBITZER's work
(L. 4940). Further, two dolls are also mentioned, representing men on ski, (L. 4900—01); these are not included
in the published list. The Museum has also received 1 drum
(L. 4857), 5 undressed figures (L. 4878—82) including one
jointed doll (vide p. 403) and four bone beads (L. 4949—50)
which articles are not mentioned either in the list delivered
to the Museum or in that now published. Finally, to complete the references made in the work to illustrations there
given of objects in the collection, the following numbers, with
those of the figures corresponding should be added:

12 (Fig. 152c), 13 (Fig. 186a), 24 (Fig. 253e), 25—35 (Fig.
253i), 36—38 (Fig. 285f and g), 43—44 (Figs. 321f and 322b),
46 (Fig. 324b), 52—53 (Fig. 180b) and 71—78 (Fig. 378a).

Among objects shown in the illustrations but not mentioned
in the published list, we have also: One Umiak cleaner (Fig.
83a) beads (Figs. 343a and b) and 1 drum (Fig. 360a).

Mr. THALBITZER evidently attaches considerable importance to his
collection, since he has seen fit to include a catalogue of the same in his
work, at the expense of HOLM's and JOHAN PETERSEN's, which are of
far greater value; it would therefore be reasonable to expect that the
catalogue given should be correct. The collection was not delivered to
the Museum until three years after his return from Greenland; and
one might suppose that he would thus have had sufficient time to
make himself fairly well acquainted with the material which he had
brought over. Nevertheless, his illustrations show no less than 15 objects
from this, his own collection, here attributed to others. Had he wished
to refresh his memory, or to fill up possible lacunae in his notes, he could
at any time have inspected the whole of the material at the Museum.
The most correct method of proceeding would have been to draw up a
list from the records of the Museum, or at any rate, to make sure that
the list to be published agreed, either with the contents of the collection
as preserved in the Museum, or with the list which accompanied it on
delivery. The third list which now appears in his work serves no good
purpose; rather, indeed, the reverse.

CONCLUDING REMARKS.

We have in the foregoing considered various typical instances of Mr. THALBITZER's peculiar methods of dealing with museum material and with such sources of information as are afforded by previously published works. We have seen that he is not always thoroughly familiar with the subjects of which he treats, and that his lack of proper qualification in this respect also makes itself apparent in his new edition of HOLM's work, included in the same volume; that he is apt to be remarkably inaccurate in quoting his authorities, and inclined now and then to formulate far-fetched conclusions on the basis of inadequate observation.

All questions such as might form the subject of scientific discussion have been purposely omitted here, only indisputable errors being dealt with. Mere inaccuracies of the mental process and of exposition have also been passed over. By way of illustration, and to save the reader, if possible, from overmuch pondering upon obscure passages, a single instance of the Author's style may here be given.

With regard to Capt. AMDRUP's find of the so-called "dead house" at Nualuk, we read, on p. 323; "The objects found were first brought by boat down to Ammassalik, where several of them were recognised as belonging to a man, who with some other families had journeyed northwards two years previous to HOLM's arrival, without anything being heard of the whole party later. The circumstances attending the discovery indicated, that the natives (over 30) had been overcome by a catastrophe, hunger or more probably poisoning from rotten meat".

And immediately after: "They had not gone much more than 80 miles from their tribal relatives, which agrees with the fact, that the ruin found was of recent date in its appearance. Although the collection found in the ruin originated from the time before the arrival of Europeans, the contents showed distinct signs of an indirect connection with European culture". (Here follow some examples). "In other respects, it confirms in every way the typological characteristics of the Ammassalik culture, which we knew from the HOLM collection. For example, there is a precise agreement between the forms of the harpoon heads in the two collections, so that we become convinced, that the types of harpoons, contained in the HOLM collection, had been fixed and predominant in this region probably for many generations".

It is not easy to see why the harpoon heads carried by a man setting out from Angmagsalik in 1882 should be expected to differ in any essential degree from those obtained by HOLM at the same place in 1884.

The sentence: "They had not gone much more than 80 miles from their tribal relatives, which agrees with the fact, that the ruin found was of recent date in its appearance" likewise furnishes food for thought. It would surely seem obvious, that the farther the party went, the later would they build, and the newer would the resulting house appear, while on the other hand, the shorter their journey, the earlier — and older — their house.

I find some difficulty also, in accepting, as does Mr. Thalbitzer, the resemblance between the harpoon heads of 1882 and those of 1884 as proof that the types "had been fixed and predominant in this region probably for many generations".

In the foregoing, I have sought to point out instances of the various difficulties which the scientific enquirer is liable to encounter, and to emphasise the need of caution in the face of errors and inaccuracies which might otherwise prove misleading. To go through the whole of the work would demand a disproportionate amount of space. For further convenience, a list of some two hundred and fifty corrections, embracing 385 pages of the book (pp. 369—753) is given in the following, arranged in order of page numbers, with references to the foregoing in such cases as have been dealt with already. Even this list, however, can make no claim to completeness.

Yet with this we might well conclude, had it not been for the fact that Mr. Thalbitzer has endeavoured to make the National Museum responsible for the quality of his work. An accusation of so serious a nature cannot be allowed to pass unrefuted. It has been pointed out in the foregoing, and — albeit the fact would seem obvious enough in itself — may here be repeated, that Mr. Thalbitzer had every opportunity of studying the entire contents of the Museum as closely and as frequently as he might wish, and that he would, on application, have been furnished with every information obtainable from the records of the Museum. He has also formerly availed himself of these opportunities, as may be seen from p. 658 of his work. It has also been shown (pp. 385—93) that Mr. Thalbitzer's method of work when dealing with written or printed sources of information entirely resembles his treatment of museum material. Further proof will be afforded by a glance at the manner in which he handles such material when undisturbed by such hindrances as he claims to have met with in the Museum, and at the results which he attains by such study.

We may take, for instance, a couple of examples from his work on the first part of the Amdrup collection[1]. Mr. Thalbitzer had here, as he himself tells us, the objects in question laid out before him all the time on a table in one of the rooms of the Kgl. Danske Videnskabernes Selskab. And as another point in his favour, we may choose out examples from the first chapters of the book, comprising 1) harpoon heads, 2) other weapon heads made of bone and 3) stone implements. At the conclusion of these sections, the Editor himself informs

---

[1] Medd. om Grønl., vol. 28, p. 329 ff. (i. e. Thalb. I).

us that he has "treated of three kinds of Eskimo implements which have hitherto been the object of particular attention on the part of ethnographers"[1]; he has thus had the work of other writers as a guide if needful. As regards the remainder, he has not had the advantage of such aids, and restricts himself also to a merely geographical arrangement of the material.

It is only fair to remark that these chapters are at least richly illustrated; 6 out of the 9 harpoon heads shown are shown three or four times each. This does not mean that they are presented from as many different points of view; the difference is in several instances restricted to the background, which is in one case white, in another black; the white makes the better picture. In Fig. 14, p. 381, we have a flake of stone, seen from two sides, concerning which the Editor observes in the text: "The specimen shows no trace of polishing or finishing so that it is uncertain whether it is an artefact at all, and whether it has ever been in use".

These sections are further marked by a strictly systematical order, almost too strict, perhaps, at times, as when we find, in Fig. 13 p. 381, under "Stone implements" the blade of a woman's knife, the remaining portion of which is given in Fig. 21 p. 403, in the geographically arranged part of the book.

On p. 347 we are told, with regard to one of the harpoon heads from North-East Greenland, that it "resembles very much a West Greenland type of harpoon head" in proof of which the Editor quotes SVENANDER[2] 40, Fig. 4. The resemblance to the illustration in question is certainly striking; SVENANDER tells us, however, expressly, on the opposite page (p. 41), that Fig. 4 represents one of the objects collected by Dr. HAMMAR in North-East Greenland. The resemblance is thus rendered less remarkable, and the connection with West Greenland disappears. With regard to this same harpoon head, we are further informed that the blade "as is "(sic) "seems, was also wedged into the slit with small pieces of iron".

Here again, I am unable to concur in Mr. THALBITZER's opinion; the present appearance of the object is due to splitting of the metal through the action of rust, a phenomenon very generally known.

The fragments from a tow-line, presented in illustration as points of Ituartit harpoons, have been dealt with in the foregoing: it only remains to add that the Editor might have avoided this, as well as other errors, if he had been content to keep to the matter in hand, instead of dragging in extraneous museum objects. And if Mr. THALBITZER had omitted the passage on p. 448 to the effect that the Norwegian ethno-

---

[1] THALB. I, p. 386.

[2] GUSTAF SVENANDER: Harpun-, Kastpil- och Lansspetsar från Väst-Grönland. Uppsala och Stockholm 1906 (Kungl. Vetenskapsakademiens handlingar Band 40, No. 3).

grapher Dr. O. SOLBERG "does not mention the three bone heads of
adzes in PFAFF's collection in the Riksmuseum at Stockholm" no one
would have suspected what we now know to be the case, that Mr. THAL-
BITZER was ignorant of the fact that an Eskimo adze-head is not bored
to receive a haft, or cut away obliquely at the hinder end with socket
at same. In other words, he would have spared himself the embarrass-
ment of confusing an adze-head with the head of a whaling harpoon —
and the harpoon head in general is a subject to which he devotes especial
attention.

Mr. THALBITZER is hardly more fortunate in his determination of
the object shown in Fig. 8 of his work. The illustration shows it as an
arrowhead: the text accompanying it, however, does not lead the reader
to any definite conclusion. "I have not been able" we read, "to find
either in MASON, MURDOCH, or NELSON any arrow the head of which
resembles this specimen from East Greenland". Arrowheads from Boòthia,
King William's Land and Alaska are then discussed, until we come to
the following: "However, among the numerous varieties of bone arrows
in the National Museum at Copenhagen there are several which resemble
that treated of here pretty closely". SOLBERG is quoted in support of
this; but even now, the Editor is not satisfied with the result,
and goes on to say: "It is, however, by no means out of the question
that we have to do with the head of a bird-dart". Some space is then
devoted to the consideration of various objects which SVENANDER rightly
states are not bird spear heads, after which we are shown an illustration
of the true head of this weapon; the specimen shown is, however, as
widely different from AMDRUP's as well may be. I leave it to the reader
himself to judge of these two objects and the accompanying text; it
would be waste of time to devote further space to the subject here.

The object in question is, then, finally shown to be the head of a
bird dart? No! not altogether. "Another, though less probable, sup-
position is that this bone head may have been used as a salmon spear,
for fishing on the ice; cf. NELSON (Alaska)". We are then told of a spear
from the Gjøa collection, intended for "salmon-spearing from a kaiak";
these spears are, however, according to Mr. THALBITZER's own words,
furnished with detachable point. And in conclusion, we read: "However,
as inv. ADM. 17 is not arranged so as to form a detachable fore-piece,
it is not quite justifiable to compare it with these western fish-spears,
especially, as fish-spears with detachable heads, as far as I know,
are not known from any district in Greenland".

And here the discussion closes, somewhat, no doubt, to the reader's
relief, since each new hypothesis, as the Editor himself admits, has proved
more improbable than the one before. It would perhaps have been
more considerate had Mr. THALBITZER expunged the hypotheses which
did not satisfy himself before sending the manuscript to print; it seems,
however, that he is afflicted with a habit of thinking aloud, for we en-

counter the same thing in the case of the next figure (Fig. 9) here reproduced for the sake of convenience as Fig. 5. With regard to these bone
heads we are told: "At first sight they look like weapon heads, but *what
kind* of weapon heads? They cannot have been detachable, loose, harpoon heads[1] belonging to the common sealing harpoons, or *agdligak*
harpoons, or to the somewhat heavier walrusing harpoons; against both
these possibilities militates .... etc.". And again "They have no slits
for blades, and thus cannot have been the fore-pieces of sealing lances.
Nor do they look like the fixed bone heads of bird darts; a
partial resemblance to the head of an arrow from Alaska ....
must be regarded as a coincidence. On the other hand, the
resemblance of these heads to the firmly secured bone heads
at the end of whaling-harpoons of the type known from
Alaska and from Baffin Land, is unmistakable. But a remarkable point about them is their small size, which might lead
one to suppose that they were only used as toys, or as models
for boys to practise with".

The discussion of these weapon heads in 1909 has, at
least, one advantage over the treatment of the arrow heads,
to wit, the fact that it ends with a definite result. In Mr.
THALBITZER's work of 1914[2], however, where the same articles
are dealt with, we read: "In my earlier description of AMDRUP's
finds from northern East Greenland I identified two cylindrical
bone points from Cape Tobin as, miniature bone fore-pieces
of whaling harpoons'. It seems more correct to regard these
as fragments of ordinary loose shafts intended to be spliced
together with thicker (lower) parts of the shaft, which are
wanting. They should thus be called, fragmentary fore-pieces
or loose shafts for harpoons'. These spliced bone shafts are
extemely common at Ammassalik".

The Editor has himself spent some time at Angmagsalik,
and has there, as he informs us, had opportunities of acquiring first-hand knowledge of the implements. The reader cannot,

Fig. 5.

$1/2$.

therefore, hesitate to believe that the front portion of these
spliced foreshafts is of the form shown in Fig. 5, viz; 1) having
a hole in front of the oblique surface, and 2) lacking the holes opposite
the oblique surface through which the two pieces of the foreshaft
are nailed together. As matters stand, however, I for my part venture
to opine, until the contrary is proved, that these pieces must be
formed after the manner of that shown by Mr. THALBITZER in Fig.
119a[3], i. e. with holes through the obliquely cut portion by means of
which the two parts can be firmly joined together, but without

---

[1] "Loose shafts" is probably was is meant.
[2] THALB. II, p. 416.
[3] THALB. II, p. 421.

any complete perforation above, which also agrees with the specimens of this nature preserved in the Museum (cf. Fig. 6), whereas
none of the alternative construction have been brought over as yet.
If this be the case, then we are still without a final conclusion of the
discussion regarding Fig. 5. And if I may be permitted to offer a hint,
I would suggest that Mr. THALBITZER in his next work should consider
the possibility of ice harpoons.

Fig. 6. $^1/_2$.

The instance above quoted will doubtless suffice to
show that the treatment of the material, and the results
arrived at, are very similar to what we find in the author's
last published work. The latter is, indeed, possibly superior
in some respects; Captain AMDRUP, for instance, had been
careful to obtain reliable information on the spot, as to
the uses of the implements in his collection, in addition
to which Mr. THALBITZER has here had the advantage of
being able, during a period of two years, to draw upon
the firsthand knowledge of so experienced an authority as
Kolonibestyrer JOHAN PETERSEN[1].

The foregoing observations have been mainly concerned with the scientific side of Cand. THALBITZER'S
work. I cannot however refrain from adding a few words
concerning his reference to the Museum with which I am
connected, and which he has made use of for the purposes
of his work, albeit, as we have seen, to so slight a degree,
and in a manner so peculiar, as greatly to impair the
scientific value of his work as a whole.

On p. 328, we are told that "only a part" of the
Greenland collections "are said to have been set up in
cases"; the reader will, however, look in vain for any definite statement as to who has "said" so. The Museum
authorities, of whom it would be most natural to enquire,
have certainly never said anything of the kind. The fact
of the matter is, that since the general rearrangement of
the collections, made some ten years back, 1) all the Greenland objects
are fully exposed for scientific inspection in the gallery set apart for this
section 2) with the exception of supplementary specimens and fragments
from the finds made on the sites of Eskimo villages, which are placed
in the window cupboards[2], everything is set out in glass cases where

---

[1] THALB. II, p. 324.

[2] These cases, which, it need hardly be said, are likewise accessible for scientific inspection, contain only matters of little importance to the scientist,
and nothing at all belonging to either HOLM's, AMDRUP's, JOHAN PETER-
SEN's or THALBITZER's collection. With regard to HOLM's collection, Mr.
THALBITZER states in one place, with a somewhat ambiguous expression,
that it "has lain" in the Museum since 1888; this is, however, according to
a later written statement of the Author himself, to be understood as mea-
ning that is has been on exhibition since that time.

the contents would be easily visible. 3) Newly received contributions are placed on view as soon as the necessary registration, etc. has been made. Immediately before the rearrangement above mentioned, and during the course of same, a number of objects were necessarily removed from their places and stored elsewhere: this took place, however, prior to the period of Mr. THALBITZER's ethnographical work[1].

The rearrangement included the procuring of much-needed space through the fitting up of a gallery 24 metres long, consisting of five deep divisions, the interjacent portions reaching nearly to the glass partition. The accompanying illustration shows the arrangement in the case of a part of the Angmagsalik collection. The left side of the picture gives one of the deep divisions, where small implements are seen lying immediately behind the glass, while the background is occupied by hunting dresses, larger implements, and sledges. The photograph, taken on a cloudy day in October 1914 by the same photographer who carried out the work for Mr. THALBITZER, shows very clearly the dresses on the wall at the back. The left half of the picture shows, on the right, the side wall of the same division, occupied by a row of spears, and in the centre one of the projecting portions, while to the left again, the adjacent division, containing West Greenland objects, is partly seen. The labels on the front edge of the shelves give descriptive notes as to the exhibits there; at the back of the deeper portion, however, numbers only are placed, the descriptive labels corresponding being set up in a frame outside the case. The strip of wood running down the centre of the picture is the framepost against which the doors rest when closed, screwed fast against a lining of soft leather, on account of the poisonous chemicals used to preserve the numerous furs against moth.

It is this arrangement to which Mr. THALBITZER refers when he tells us that "The Greenland objects are placed in unusually deep glass cases, in which it is almost impossible for the visitor to see what is placed at the back and in which most of the objects can only be got at with great difficulty". As regards the first part of this statement, the reader can himself judge, from the accompanying photograph, taken at a considerably greater distance from the case than that at which the visitor ordinarily would stand, how far it may be justified. As regards the latter

---

[1] Unreasonable as it would seem, it is nevertheless not improbable that the Author's "are said" refers to this remote period, since, in a note on the same page, he harks back to the last century in order to draw attention to an alleged neglect on the part of the Museum authorities in connection with a request made to them. My own connection with the Museum Ethnographical Collections does not date back so far as include any personal knowledge of this ancient matter; I must therefore confine myself to the suggestion that since the gentleman concerned — an eminent American ethnographer, now long since deceased — did not think fit to carry the matter farther after receiving the letter forwarded by the Museum authorities under date 21.—6.—1897, then surely Mr. THALBITZER also would have done well to let it rest.

part, it should be mentioned that the whole interior furniture of the cases consists of loose shelves, which can be removed at any time with their contents. They were also thus removed for Mr. THALBITZER's convenience, and placed outside, where he could freely select and study his material.

The whole of this arrangement, with its alternating deep divisions, the movable shelves and large doors reaching from floor to ceiling, which can be drawn right back to the glass partition, has been commended by experts as an exceptionally happy solution of the problem: given a restricted amount of space, to obtain a scientifically adequate arrangement of the collections, rendering them at the same time thoroughly comprehensible for the ordinary visitor and easily accessible for the scientist.

Mr. THALBITZER then goes on to say that he "obtained very little time to study the objects taken from the cases, as they had to be brought out and put in again each day by one of the assistants". It is perfectly true, that the replacing of removed shelves at the end of each working day is one of the constant rules of the Museum. This is necessary, both for the preservation of the objects themselves, and for the convenience of the general public, and there can be no reasonable grounds for complaint when the same shelves are brought out next day by one of the staff to the same place where they had been placed for inspection on the foregoing. The research student would, on the other hand, have every reason to complain if the Museum authorities did not accord him sufficient time to prosecute his investigations: on this point again, however, Mr. THALBITZER's statement is altogether at variance with the actual facts. He was of course at liberty to have the same shelves removed for inspection as often as he might desire. Mr. THALBITZER has here evidently used an ill-chosen expression; it cannot have been his intention to say what his words imply.

With regard to his work in the Museum, Mr. THALBITZER further states: "I directed a request therefore in 1908 to the Director of the ethnographical section, Dr. SOPHUS MÜLLER, that I might be permitted to study the collections from East Greenland and first and foremost G. HOLM's. In the following year I asked to be allowed to photograph HOLM's collection. In the spring of 1910 I succeeded at length in beginning the work of photographing which extended over 16 days".

It must be admitted that this passage, taken sentence by sentence, is perfectly in accordance with the truth; here again, however, Mr. THALBITZER has been unfortunate in his choice of expression; his words as they stand might well be construed as meaning that the writer had spent a couple of years in vain endeavours to obtain permission to photograph and study the collections. This is far from being the case. Only in a single instance did Mr THALBITZER meet with any hindrance on the part of the Museum authorities, viz. in the case of his application in June 1909 for permission to photograph. Here the authorities were obliged to defer the desired permission for three months, the Museum being during that time open daily to the public, so that the rooms in question could not be reserved for special work. The fact that Mr. THALBITZER chose to wait until the 24th of February of the following year cannot be laid to the charge of the Museum.

Mr. THALBITZER tells us that he employed "a photographer recommended by the director" and that the work of photographing was carried out "in front of the cases, where the light conditions were not exactly good" and "somewhat hastily owing to the short working hours of the museum". It should here be observed, that although the Museum authorities furnished Mr. THALBITZER with the name of a photographer having considerable experience of photographic work in the Museum, he was perfectly at liberty to engage another had he pleased; further, that the photographer in question has declared in writing that the light was satisfactory, and that the working hours accorded — from 10 or 12 to 4 — were fully sufficient to permit of the work being done clearly and well.

It will thus be seen that Mr. THALBITZER has had full liberty to prosecute his studies in the Museum, the only restrictions being such as would inveritably arise from the regulations to which every student must necessarily be expected to conform. Since, however, he has been unable to realise the necessity of such restrictions, but has construed them as unfriendliness, and now endeavours to bring the Danish National Museum into ill repute abroad, the Museum authorities are forced to correct and explain the frequently vague and misleading statements in which he expresses himself. Mr. THALBITZER evidently fails to realise the fact that a Museum accessible to and much visited by the general public cannot altogether set aside the interests of the ordinary visitor in order to serve the convenience of a single investigator.

Finally, we read: "I regret that such a short measure of interest and friendliness obliged me to renounce a fuller utilization of the rich collections and has thus without doubt reduced the strength of my work". In the face of this repeated accusation, we must once more emphatically assert that Mr. THALBITZER might to the full have utilised the collections for the purposes of his work, and I will take upon myself to point out, that it was his plain duty as a scientist to utilise the Danish Museum to the highest possible degree, the more so since it is there, and not in the foreign Museums he mentioned, that the material which was to form the subject of his work was to be found. Had he, as he gives his readers to understand, encountered opposition on the part of the Museum in the prosecution of his studies, two courses would have lain open to him: either to request the Committee which had entrusted him with the work to intervene, or to declare that he could not, under the circumstances, undertake to complete the task. The course which he has adopted:

of publishing his work on the basis of highly inadequate study of his subject, and afterwards seeking to lay the blame on the Museum, carries its own condemnation.

The fact that the work in question has been accorded a place among the "Meddelelser om Grønland" which stand in so high repute as scientific publications, renders it impossible to disregard it altogether; the title in question is very properly regarded in scientific circles as conferring a patent of reliability. As a matter of fact, however, it should be borne in mind that the editors of the series do not hold themselves responsible for the contents of the volumes, and the individual author's selection of quotations, his treatment of literary sources, his description of objects and statements concerning their origin are thus likewise outside the Committee's control.

Since the foregoing was written, other works have appeared bearing in part upon the same points, and in certain respects supplementing the observations therein contained. It will therefore be proper to call attention to the publications in question. They are as follows:

> Nordisk Tidskrift för Vetenskap, Konst och Industri, 1914, pp. 530—34, a review by GUDMUND HATT.
> Meddelelser om Grønland, vol. 51; MORTEN P. PORSILD, Studies on the material culture of the Eskimo in West Greenland.
> Det Grønlandske Selskabs Aarsskrift 1915, pp. 62—71, a review by KAJ BIRKET-SMITH.

The editors of Meddelelser om Grønland having intimated that a reply from Cand. THALBITZER will be published in the same volume as the present work, and that the discussion, as far as the periodical in question is concerned, will therewith be considered closed, I take this opportunity of mentioning that a further statement on my part may, if deemed necessary, be expected to appear in a Danish or English periodical.

Finally, I beg to express my best thanks to the Carlsberg Fund, which has borne the expenses of the foregoing work.

CORRECTIONS TO W. THALBITZER'S ETHNOGRAPHICAL COLLECTIONS FROM EAST GREENLAND.

Page.

369. L. 3; "ornamental expansions". These expansions are not ornaments, but are of practical importance, being intended to strengthen those parts where the pull of the thong is felt.

380. Fig. 83 a (Mus. No. L. 4940) was not brought over by HOLM, but by W. THALBITZER 1906.

Page.

383. L. 15—16. "Kayaks have been used everywhere naturally" Among the Polar Eskimos the kayak was at any rate not in use during the period 1818 to about 1860.

388. Fig. 92c (Mus. No. L. b. 695) was not brought over by HOLM, but by RYDER 1892.

389. Line 20; "bird's claw". The bird in question is a polar bear. Line 2 from below: "bow". NELSON, from whom the quotation is taken, gives "board" which makes better sense.

390. L. 4. "Various other small variations of this type also occur in Alaska. cf. NELSON l. c. Pl. LXXIX fig. 4 and MASON (1900) Pl. XIV". It is the same object (Washington Museum No. 160. 337) in both cases, and is not a small variation, but an entirely distinct implement, which cannot be used as a float and which stands on three legs rising above the kayak itself.

408. Fig. 103b (Mus. No. L. 1555) was not brought over by HOLM, but by JOHAN PETERSEN 1897. Fig. 104 is a child's harpoon. Figs. 105 and 106a—b (L.b. 688 [1] and L.b. 687 [1-2] respectively) were brought over by RYDER.

411. Cf. PORSILD p. 240—41.

418. Cf. PORSILD p. 241.

420. Figs. 116a (L.b. 686) and 118a (L.b. 678) were not brought over by HOLM, but by RYDER 1892. In the case of 116a, this correction should also be made in the text p. 419.

425. Cf. PORSILD p. 240.

432. Cf. PORSILD p. 240.

435. Fig. 137a, b, c (Mus. No. L.b. 689[1-3]) Figs. 139a (L.b. 685), 139b (L.b. 684) and 140b (L.b. 683) were all brought over by RYDER 1892. Fig. 140a, which belongs to the HOLM collection, has three teeth, the middle one must have been missing when the piece was photographed, as all three teeth are still in position.

439. Fig. 144 (Mus. No. L.b. 367) is part of a child's harpoon. The scale, stated as "$1/_8$?" should be altered to $1/_5$.

454. Fig. 152. The specimen farthest to the left, (Mus. No. L.c. 1335) was brought home by C. RYDER 1892; No. 3 from the left (Mus. No. L. 4944) by W. THALBITZER 1906.

455. In Fig. 154, the kayak stand belongs to RYDER's collection (L.b. 695[2]); the remainder is difficult to identify. The scale "$1/_{14}$?" should be $1/_8$. As to the double bladder cf. PORSILD p. 242.

458. Fig. 158. All six specimens (a—f) are from RYDER's collection 1892 (Mus. No. L.b. 659[1-6]); the same applies to Fig. 159c (L.b. 673[2]).

460. Fig. 161. This specimen is from JOHAN PETERSEN 1897 (Mus. No. L. 1555). The scale is stated as "$1/_{10}$?". $1/_{10}$ is correct, and the query may therefore be deleted.

465. Figs. 172a (Mus. No. L.b. 658[1]) and 172b (L.b. 670) are both from C. RYDER's voyage of 1892.

Page.

467. Fig. 174 (L.b. 661) was brought over by RYDER 1892.

468. Fig. 175b (L.b. 671[1]) likewise brought over by RYDER 1892.

471. Fig. 180b (L. 4920) was brought over by W. THALBITZER 1906.

473. Fig. 181b (L.b. 660[1]) is from C. RYDER's voyage of 1892, as also Fig. 182f (L.c. 1293).

476. Fig. 186 left (L. 4848) is from W. THALBITZER's voyage 1906; correction should also be made in text p. 475.

Linie 15—27. OLEARIUS' statement is misunderstood. The knives from Southampton Island have stone, not iron blades (*vide supra* pp. 404—05).

Note 6. The illustration in GRAAH's work is Pl. VIII, not VII.

477. Fig. 187b (L.c. 371) was not brought over by HOLM, but was found by GRAAH as far back as 1829 at Malingiset, on the East coast of Greenland, Lat. 62°20′ N. The scale of Fig. 187 is not $1/_6$ but $1/_5$.

Fig. 188b (L.c. 1291[1]) was brought over by C. RYDER 1892.

478. Fig. 189 is not a hammer, but a chisel (*vide supra* pp. 398—99).

Fig. 190 is not a drill, but a whetting iron (*vide supra* pp. 396—97).

479. Fig. 191c (L. 1495) was collected by JOHAN PETERSEN 1897.

480. Line 1; *vide supra* pp. 396—97 L. 2 "likewise" should be deleted, as the former of the two objects was not brough tover by HOLM.

Fig. 192b (L.c. 896) was presented in 1883 by Konferentsraad RYBERG: it was procured from East Greenlanders, but is hardly from Angmagsalik. Figs. 192c and d (L. 1506[1] and L. 1506[6]) were brought over by Joh. PETERSEN 1897.

481. Lines 8—9. Finger and knee protectors are also used on the West Coast.

482. Fig. 195, the scale is incorrectly stated; should be $1/_2$.

489. Note 1. PEARY has brought home 3 meteorites to America (cf. Meddel. om Grønland vol. 32, p. 513).

496. Figs. 205a and b (L. 4446 and 4447). Presented by JOHAN PETERSEN 1909. c. (L.c. 1296) brought over by RYDER 1892. 205d-g and 206a-b we have been unable to identify. If preserved in the National Museum, it must be presumed that they are from West Greenland: they are in any case insignificant fragments.

497. Lines 21 ff. As the objects shown in Fig. 206 cannot be identified it is impossible to say whether a. is a scraper; this cannot be seen from the illustration b. is a fragment of one of the flakes of stone which are of very frequent occurrence in West Greenland: they are found in hundreds, especially in the same small size. It is not likely that any important archæological results can be obtained from this.

499. L. 25; The point shown in Fig. 210l is of bone, not of slate.

501. Cf. PORSILD p. 246.

502. Fig. 218a-b (L.c. 1292[2] and 1292[1]) were brought home by RYDER 1892. Fig. 218c is not a whetstone, but a whetting iron (cf. *supra* pp. 397—98).

Page.

508. Fig. 223e (L. 4414) was presented by JOHAN PETERSEN in 1909.

509. Line 3 from below. The object shown in Fig. 223d has a red bead inset in the wooden handle on the side not visible in the picture.

Line 2 from below. Fig. 223e had a wooden handle, with iron arms and blade. The arms in Fig. 223f however, are of bone.

512. Fig. 231a is, it is true, mentioned by HOLM as a skin creaser; it was, however, doubtless originally intended as a toggle on some line which passed through the hole bored from one side to the other (cf. Fig. 531c).

Fig. 234a (L.b. 657[1]) was brought over by RYDER 1892.

517. Fig. 241. Text to illustration amended under corrigenda as follows: "guard .... guard (HOLM coll.) $^1/_2$". This scale is not correct; it should be abt. $^1/_5$ (cf. *supra* p. 403).

Fig. 242a (L.c. 1299) brought home by RYDER 1892.

521. Fig. 249a (L.c. 1302) and c (L.c. 1305) likewise from RYDER 1892.

522. Fig. 250b (L.c. 1303) brought over by RYDER 1892; c (L. 1503) from JOHAN PETERSEN 1897.

528. Figs. 253a, d and f are from HOLM's collection; b. and c. from RYDER's, e. and i. brought over by W. THALBITZER in 1906, h. presented by Pastor C. RÜTTEL 1903.

529. Fig. 254b is from HOLM's collection, a and d are from RYDER's, c. is from JOHAN PETERSEN 1897.

531. Fig. 256b (L. 4429) presented by JOHAN PETERSEN 1909, together with the strap belonging to the "fire-making implement" shown in Fig. 256c, the remaining portions of which are from HOLM's collection. The lamp moss marked e. is from RYDER's collection (L.c. 1353).

533. Fig. 258. Only the wick trimmer placed in the lamp marked b. belongs to the HOLM collection: a-c. (L. 4426, 4423 and 4422) were presented by JOHAN PETERSEN 1909, while d. (L.c. 1350) is from RYDER's expedition of 1892.

534. Fig. 260. Only the drying frame a. is from the HOLM collection. The cooking pot b. (L.c. 1349[1]) and the lamp with stand d. (L.c. 1350—51) belong to Ryder's collection.

544. Fig. 263a (L.c. 1324) was brought home by RYDER 1892; b. (L.c. 937) by HOLM 1885.

Fig. 264 (L.c. 954[1]) is a model.

546. Fig. 271a (L.c. 964[1]). Scale ($^1/_4$) incorrect; should be abt $^1/_2$. The length of the specimen is 17 cm.

Fig. 271b (L.c. 1329[1]) is not from HOLM's but from RYDER's collection; the scale is not $^1/_4$ but a little under $^1/_2$.

Fig. 271c (L. 4419) was presented in 1909 by JOHAN PETERSEN; the scale is abt. $^1/_3$.

Fig. 271d-g are reproduced to scale abt. $^2/_7$, not $^1/_4$; only f and

Page.

g. (L.c. 963$^{1-2}$) are from HOLM's collection, e. (L.c. 1328) being from RYDER's, and d. (L. 1518) sent by JOHAN PETERSEN 1897.

547. Fig. 272. Both (L.c. 1326$^{1-2}$) brought over by RYDER.

Fig. 273 (L.c. 268) sent over in 1849 by Kolonibestyrer KIELSEN (*vide supra* p. 393 ff.).

550. Fig. 276. Both the objects are models, a. (L.c. 1341) was brought over by C. RYDER in 1892.

Fig. 277 is a model.

Fig. 279 (L.c. 1546) was brought over in 1897 by JOHAN PETERSEN.

551. Fig. 280a (L.c. 1340) was brought over by RYDER 1892.

Fig. 280b (L.c. 959^1) is a model; the scale given is incorrect, and should be, not $^1/_{10}$, but abt. $^1/_6$.

Fig. 280c (L.c. 267) was sent over in 1849 together with the specimen shown in Fig. 273 by Kolonibestyrer KIELSEN (*vide supra* p. 393 ff.).

352. Fig. 281b is not a drinking cup, but a blubber pot.

553. Fig. 283b (L. 2060) was presented by Pastor C. Rüttel 1903.

555. Fig. 285f and g (L. 4829 and 4828) were brought over by W. THALBITZER 1906.

556. Fig. 286b and j (L.c. 1345^1 and L.c. 1344^1) are from RYDER's collection 1892; c. and m. (L. 1517 and L. 1516) were sent over by JOHAN PETERSEN 1897.

560. Figs. 289a and d (L.c. 1323$^{1-2}$) brought over by RYDER 1892; e. (L. 4432) presented by JOHAN PETERSEN in 1909.

564. Fig. 291. None of these objects are from HOLM's collection, a. (L.d. 120^1) was brought over by RYDER 1892, b. (L. 1536^1) sent over by JOHAN PETERSEN 1897.

565. Fig. 292. Of these again, neither is from HOLM's collection, a. (L.d. 133^1) is from RYDER's voyage of 1892, b. (L. 4393) was presented in 1909 by JOHAN PETERSEN.

567. Fig. 293. Here again, nothing from HOLM's collection. a. (L. 4396) was presented in 1909 by JOHAN PETERSEN, b. (L.d. 132^1) is from RYDER's collection of 1892. These are, however, at least from Angmagsalik, which is not the case with the following: c. (L.d. 6) presented by Kolonibestyrer HØYER 1865, and d. (L.c. 222) presented by Inspektør HOLBØLL 1846 (*vide supra* p. 388).

569. Fig. 295. The dress (L.d. 119 etc.) was brought over by RYDER 1892, with the exception of the shoes, which are from the HOLM collection.

572—3. Figs. 296—297. This dress (L. 1531 etc.) is from JOHAN PETERSEN 1897.

574. Fig. 298. The dress (L.d. 118 etc.) was brought over by RYDER 1892. As to frocks of bird's skin cf. PORSILD p. 246.

582. Fig. 304 (L.d. 130 etc.) brought over by RYDER 1892.

Page.

583. None of the garments shown in Figs. 305—307 are from HOLM's collection: 305 (L. 1541 and 1535) being from JOHAN PETERSEN 1897; 306 and 307 (L.d. 129—30 and 133) from RYDER's expedition of 1892.

584. Fig. 308. The specimen b. we have been unable to identify. The border on the lower edge shows that it cannot be identical with a.

585. Fig. 309. The garments are not from HOLM's collection; they are separate items received between 1849—54 and originate from southern East Greenland. The frock (L.c. 271) was presented by Kolonibestyrer KIELSEN in 1849, the breeches (L.c. 373) being the gift of H. RINK 1854 and the boots (L.c. 310) from HOLBØLL 1850.

586. The child's dress Fig. 310 (L.d. 131 etc.) is from RYDER's collection.
     The boots Fig. 311a-b (L. 4399 and 4398) were presented by JOHAN PETERSEN 1909.

587. Fig. 312 received in 1897 from JOHAN PETERSEN (L. 1533).

589. Of the objects shown in Fig. 314, only b. (L.d. 60) is from HOLM's collection; a. (L. 1542) was sent over by JOHAN PETERSEN 1897, while c. and d: (L.d. 140[1] and 146) belong to RYDER's collection.

591. Of the caps shown in Fig. 315 b. and c. (L.d.138[1-2]) are from RYDER's collection, while e. and g. (L. 1543) were received from JOHAN PETERSEN 1897.

593. Of the eye-shades shown in Fig. 316 only half are from the HOLM collection, and of the remaining 5, only one, viz. that marked k. (L.d. 145) is from Angmagsalik, this being brought over by RYDER 1892. The other four are of earlier date and were procured from Julianehaab, whither they had been brought by natives from the southern East Coast; d. (L.c. 100) was presented by Kolonibestyrer KIELSEN 1840; g. (L.c. 177) by Inspektør HOLBØLL 1844; h. (L.d. 13) by Distriktslæge JESSEN 1881 and i. (4544) by Inspektør HOLBØLL in 1838.

596. Fig. 321f is from W. THALBITZER's voyage of 1906 (L. 4852).

597. Fig. 322b (L. 4851) likewise brought over by W. THALBITZER 1906.

598. Of the objects shown in Fig. 323 a. and e. (L.d. 142[1-2]) were brought over by RYDER 1892, that marked f. (L. 1526) being sent in by JOHAN PETERSEN in 1897.

599. Of the five objects shown in Figs. 324 and 325, only one, viz. 325a (L.d. 52[1]) is from HOLM's expedition of 1884—5; another, 325c (L.d. 26) was brought over by HOLM in 1881. No. 325b on the other hand (L.d. 150) is from RYDER's expedition of 1892, while 324a (L. 4404) was presented by JOHAN PETERSEN in 1909, and 324b is from W. THALBITZER's voyage 1906.

602. Fig. 327b (L. 1529) was received in 1897 from JOHAN PETERSEN.

603. Fig. 328a (L.d. 149[1]) belongs to the RYDER collection; b. (L. 4406) was presented in 1909 by JOHAN PETERSEN.

604. Fig. 330c (L.d. 151) was brought over by C. RYDER 1892.

605. Of the six combs shown in Fig. 331, only one, viz. a. (L.c. 939¹) is from HOLM's collection, those marked c., d. and e. (L.c. 1298¹⁻³) being from RYDER's, while b. and f. (L. 1505¹ and ³) were received from JOHAN PETERSEN 1897.

606. The comb in Fig. 332 is an imitation of a type of comb used at an earlier period; it was made to order for JOHAN PETERSEB.

607. Fig. 334 (L. 4431) was presented by JOHAN PETERSEN 1909.

611. Figs. 335b and d. and 339 we have been unable to identify, 338, however, noted by THALBITZER as "HOLM(?) coll." is, as a matter of fact, from RYDER's voyage of 1892 (L.c. 1337).

614. The two beads shown in the lower part of Fig. 343 we have been unable to identify; the two other items in the same Fig. however, (L. 4949 and 4950) were brought over, not by HOLM, but by W. THALBITZER, in 1906. The scale is incorrect: it should be abt. $^1/_3$.

     Of the objects shown in Fig. 344, that marked a. is from HOLM's expedition of 1884—85, and is part of the lock belonging to the wooden case shown in Fig. 289c (L.c. 979¹); b. (L.d. 26) was received from HOLM 1881.

626. Of the three amulet straps shown in Fig. 348, that marked a. (L. 1493) was received from JOHAN PETERSEN in 1897, while c. was presented by Pastor C. RÜTTEL in 1903.

632. Fig. 350a (L.a. 17) is from HOLM's expedition of 1884—85; b. (L.a. 16) is not from East Greenland, but was taken from a grave at Ungudlik in the Julianehaab district. The rest, 350c-f and 351a-c were presented by Pastor C. RÜTTEL (cf. *supra* p. 382).

633. Fig. 352 (L.c. 1338) is from RYDER's voyage of 1892.

635. Line 3 from below to p. 636 L. 8; *vide supra* p. 391 ff.

636. Line 12 from below to p. 637 L. 2; *vide supra* pp. 399—400.

641. Fig. 360a (L. 4857) was brought over by THALBITZER 1906.

     Fig. 361 "Drumsticks". These are not two distinct objects, but two presentments of the same drumstick, viewed from side and front respectively. (L.c. 904³).

645. Fig. 366 l and m. are not, as stated, made of wood, but of bone (cf. *supra* p. 400); b. (L.c. 1269⁴³) has a hairknot, later pegged down into the doll's head; this was, however, removed when the photograph was taken. The dolls marked c, f, h, i, k, l and m belong to HOLM's collection; the remainder from RYDER's.

647. Line 1—8; *vide supra* p. 402.

651. Fig. 372a-c (L.c. 1273¹⁻³) and 374a (L.c. 1313) were brought over by RYDER 1892; 374c and d (L. 1507¹⁻²) by JOHAN PETERSEN 1897.

653. Fig. 376c (L.c. 1280) ⎫
654. Fig. 377 (L.c. 1286) ⎬ are from RYDER's collection.

     Of the two puzzles shown in Fig. 378, that marked a. (L. 4945) was brought over by THALBITZER in 1906; b. is not identified, but is in any case not from the HOLM collection.

Page.

655. Fig. 379a was sent over by JOHAN PETERSEN 1897 (L. 1494).

667. Fig. 392 (L.a. 1) was received in 1848, and is not from Angmagsalik (*vide supra* p. 388) Fig. 393 (L.c. 100) is likewise not from Angmagsalik; it was presented as far back as 1865 by Kolonibestyrer HØYER.

674. Cf. PORSILD p. 246.

677. Lances vide PORSILD p. 246. "The shark's tooth knives", *vide supra* p. 405.

678. "Hammer, chisel, wedge"; *vide supra* pp. 398—99.

679. Cf. PORSILD p. 243 ff.

681. "Dolls" *vide supra* pp. 402—03.

682 ff. "Earlier authors on the Eskimo of the Davis Strait"; *vide supra* p. 389 ff.

725. Lines 11—15. The knives referred to are not, as stated, peculiar to Angmagsalik, but are also found in West Greenland.

728. On this page, reference is made to 39 "implements" or "forms and details of otherwise common types" as being peculiar to Angmagsalik. With regard to these the following should be noted:

4. Boat hooks. As to boat hooks nothing whatever is known. (cf. *supra* pp. 406—07).

5. The cross-shaped kaiak stand has, as the Editor correctly states on p. 387, also been in use in West Greenland, and should therefore not be included here.

13. Men's finger and knee protectors are likewise used in West Greenland.

16. "Old-fashioned men's knives". The expression is certainly somewhat vague; here also, however, it will doubtless be correct to remark that such articles are likewise known in West Greenland.

26. Ivory pendants as ornaments on needle skins are, it is true, only known from Angmagsalik: this is, however, merely a natural corollary to what is stated under (19), viz. that the needle skins are only found there.

39. Slings are known among the Polar Eskimos.

736. "Hough W. Fire-making apparatus etc. Report Nat. Mus. Washington 1888"; should be "Report Nat. Mus. for 1888. Washington 1890".

Similar correction should also be made in the case of all his references to W. HOUGH's and O. T. MASON's works, on pp. 736—7, whereas in the case of W. J. HOFFMAN's (p. 735) and T. WILSON's (p. 741) the date given is the year of publication.

MASON's "Aboriginal skin dressing" is noted as from Washington 1888—89; it should be Rep. for 1889, Washington 1891.

738. "NORDENSKIÖLD, A. E. Den andra Dicksonska Expeditionen etc. Stockholm 1885?" The note of interrogation may be dispensed with.

Page

     Poincy. The chapter in question is the 18th, not the 8th.

739. Ryder, C. Here should be added: Beretning om den østgrønlandske Expedition 1891—92 (Medd. om Grønl. vol. 17) this work
being also quoted by the Editor (*vide supra* pp. 400—01).

     "Schacht Manuscr. N. Kgl. S. 4° 1965 (and A. M. 364 Fol. and
A. M. 775 4°) Kbhvn. 1789". Should be: A. M. 364 Fol. Kerte-
minde 1689. The rest may be dispensed with (cf. *supra* pp.
390—91).

743—53. Lists of Amdrup's and Thalbitzer's collections: *vide* p. 410ff.

TRANSLATED BY W. J. ALEXANDER WORSTER